An Astonishing Hope

A 60-Day Devotional for Cancer Sufferers

By Phil Wicklund

8/14/25

Dear Caroline,
Hope you enjoy this book as much as I do.
Love always,
Gladi

Cover Design by JT Marshall

AstonishingHope.org

Copyright © 2023 by Phillip Wicklund

All rights reserved.

No part of this book may be reproduced or used in any manner without the written permission of the copyright owner except for the use of quotations in a book review.

ISBN: 979-8-218-39735-7

Published by The Way With Words, 1337 Greenhill Road, West Chester, PA, 19380

Unless otherwise noted, all Scripture quotations are taken from the Christian Standard Bible®, Copyright© 2017 by Holman Bible Publishers. Used by permission. Christian Standard Bible® and CSB® are federally registered trademarks of Holman Bible Publishers.

Table of Contents

Dedication 5

Foreword 7

Preface 9

Promises for Cancer Sufferers 11

Hope for Cancer Sufferers from Philippians 107

Epilogue 206

Afterword 209

Appendix 211

Acknowledgements 213

Dedication

To my wife Sarah and five children, Addy, Noah, Molly, Henry, and Ted: I pray you will always fix your eyes on Jesus, through everything, forever.

Foreword

What you are about to read is a testimony of God's astonishing power. From cancer diagnosis through treatment, Phil Wicklund shares his journey of finding his faith in God during life's hardest moments.

I've had the wonderful opportunity of walking with the Wicklund family as one of their pastors at Sanctuary Covenant Church in Minneapolis, MN. We are an urban, multi-ethnic, multiplying movement reconciling people to God and one another. They are an integral part of our community. I also grew up with Phil's wife, Sarah, attending the same school in a town outside of the Twin Cities. In getting to know Phil and his family, I've seen that this family practices what they preach and embodies the teachings of Jesus to love and serve others. This has been evident in their lives well before Phil's cancer diagnosis, but has been especially evident in the time following.

Just days after Phil's diagnosis, I remember going to their house along with elders from our church. I knew we'd spend time in prayer together and that his five children would be present. I was preparing myself for a gut-wrenching prayer session, filled with tears and sadness. What I walked into, however, was the complete opposite. While there were tears shed and fears expressed, the overwhelming tone was one of praise and trust in God. Phil shared honestly with us about his fears, but all of that was overshadowed by his immense joy in God's salvation and assurance in God's promises for his life and that of his family. This was a new and transformed person.

In the days and months that followed, Phil has been an encouragement to many. His steadfast faith and deepening confidence in God's power have been a testimony of God's grace and goodness. None of this to say that it's been easy for him and his family, but through God's Word and the Body of Christ, I am reminded again that the valley of the shadow of death is no match for God's matchless power.

In reading Phil's story, I was reminded of my own experience with loss, cancer, and renewed hope. Growing up I was diagnosed with a condition that precluded me from normal growth and development as a child. As a result, I went to the Mayo Clinic every three months for the duration of my childhood—that equals countless pokes, prods, scans, testing, and assessments. While that experience developed my own faith in unique ways, it also came with the welcomed stay with my cousin every three months, as she lived in Rochester, MN mere miles away from the Mayo Clinic. I grew very close to her and her growing family from those visits—even becoming a godmother to her youngest child when I was only in high school! While her children were still young, she received a diagnosis of breast cancer. The news was heartbreaking. She fought for many years through remission and recurrence, allowing her own faith to grow through the experience as well. Ultimately, in 2018 she died of cancer, leaving behind her husband and four children. I had the honor of officiating her funeral and sharing the hope we have in God because of Jesus. It was a significant moment for me, as I wrestled myself with the reality of death yet the hope we have in Christ. I was reminded of that same paradox of faith in reading Phil's words and his assurance in Paul's words in Philippians 1:21 where he writes, "For to me, to live is Christ and to die is gain." I pray that God's truth, expressed in these daily devotionals, will encourage your own faith in Christ, solidify the truth in God's promises, while relying on the Holy Spirit for comfort through the ups and downs of cancer.

This book is honest and raw. It is heartfelt and inspiring. I encourage you to open yourself up to God and see how he will transform your sadness into joy in what may feel like the darkest and most hopeless season of life.

Rev. Dr. Rose Lee-Norman
December 2023
Minneapolis, MN

Preface

My primary goal for this book, before it ever was a "book," was to journal my way through the promises of God and pray my way through the book of Philippians during my fiery trial of cancer. I desired to uncover the greatness of God in the Scriptures, to encourage my heart through the process, and to tear down any fear or uncertainty that God is not capable of mighty things for myself and my family, even amidst my cancer diagnosis and treatment.

I say "primary goal" because I desperately needed (and still need) these promises to sustain me. Fear and sadness ebbed and flowed continually, and I needed the word of God to penetrate me deeply so that I could fight temptation and keep my eyes on Jesus, who was and is my greatest hope. So yes, I primarily wrote this book for myself; it was my desperate attempt to walk with God through a deep dark valley.

But I also hope to leave a legacy to my children with this book. They are still quite young. I am eager to use this "opportunity" of cancer to lean into Christ and to lead in the home, to point them to Christ—for that is my most sincere hope for them, that they would believe in Jesus and stand firm in an astonishing hope, knowing God loves them. My prayer is that this book would be a way I can speak to them today in ways they may not be able to fully comprehend given their ages, but will in the future. I am eagerly awaiting the day when they will know the love of their Father, and the love of their father, completely.

Perhaps the Lord will also use these meditations to bless others outside my family, even those I've never met nor ever will. This became more and more clear to me in the process of journaling my way through cancer, that perhaps God was going to do something beyond anything I had intended. God be praised if that is what happens; to Jesus be the glory. I sincerely do desire for you, my reader, to be rooted in the astonishing hope that I have been rooted in, by God's grace.

This astonishing hope in Christ Jesus has sustained me

through diagnoses, prognoses, PET scans, CT scans, chemo, radiation, and surgery. All of those are fearful things, but even more, the hope I have in Christ has sustained me in the "in-betweens." Nothing is worse than the waiting, and I hope this book will show how you too can wait with eager expectation of God's faithfulness, instead of in fear and anxiety. Nothing will repel the spiritual attacks that accompany cancer better than the bulwark of God's steadfast love for you.

I wrote this book in two halves: 1) 30 days of promises of God for the sufferer, and 2) 30 days of hope for the sufferer from the book of Philippians. As I dove deep into the Word during my ordeal, looking for help from the Lord, I found many promises from various places in Scripture, but I also noticed that my journal entries contained more quotes from Philippians than anywhere else. The apostle Paul, who wrote Philippians, was well-acquainted with suffering. I realized that the epistle was written especially for the sufferer, and taking its pieces out of context isn't as beautiful and powerful as walking through them in order.

You'll notice that some ideas are repeated often throughout this book. That's intentional, because I think we need to be reminded again and again of them, especially when we are suffering in significant ways.

There's so much astonishing hope for us throughout the Bible and in the book of Philippians in particular. The promises of God are the sure foundation on which to stand during cancer and any other trial in life. All other ground is sinking sand.

30 Days .of Promises for Cancer Sufferers

This is a collection of God's promises that I've clung to during my walk with cancer. Some were sent to me by friends and family for encouragement and others the Lord brought to remembrance during my time of need.

I treasured and still continue to treasure them.

The promises of God are our solid rock in the storm and his rod and staff that comfort us while we walk through the valley of the shadow of death. In them God is with us, and by them he holds us in his righteous right hand.

My prayer is that you will be encouraged as I have been by these promises. You are not alone, despite how isolating cancer can be. Others have walked this path and found it to be sorrowful, yes, but also joyful, hopeful, and even by God's amazing grace, peaceful.

May it be so for you.

> *Lord God, may this experience, this suffering, and even the joys discovered through this tribulation, abound in faith, joy, hope, and peace in Jesus. For from Him and through Him and to Him are all things (Romans 11:36). Even cancer. To him be glory forever.*
>
> *In Jesus' name, Amen!*

Day 1

Fear

Isaiah 41:10, 13

So do not fear, for I am with you; do not be dismayed, for I am your God. I will strengthen you and help you; I will uphold you with my righteous right hand.... For I am the LORD, your God, who takes hold of your right hand and says to you, "Do not fear; I will help you."

(The following is the first journal entry I'd ever written in my life, on the day the doctors found a tumor in my esophagus. I left the entry in its original form because I suspect others will resonate with the fear, and hope, that I felt that desperate day.)

Today I learned that I have a "likely malignant" tumor in my esophagus. Fear is my #1 enemy at the moment. I've cried today more than the combined tears of my 40 years of life on this earth.

By God's providence, some family friends were already scheduled to come over tonight to hang out with my wife and me. They gave me these verses in Isaiah to think over. Their faith was such a blessing to us to be around—it was infectious! Their prayers for me really encouraged my heart after the hardest day of my life. Oh how I long to be so rooted in Christ Jesus as they are!

It was wonderful to be met with this verse right when I needed it. I felt the Holy Spirit pulling me toward a deeper relationship with Him, and peace, despite many tears, is slowly emerging.

Today was an unimaginably hard, long day. But I got through it and was greatly encouraged by my wife and friends.

The body of Christ is truly the hands and feet of God working in this world!

Now more than ever, I long to be surrounded by my community of believers!

Prayer to the Lord

> *Lord Jesus, drive away fear from me! I am afraid! Strengthen me! Help me! Help me not to be dismayed! Uphold me by your righteous right hand! For I need your strength; I have none for myself. You say not to fear, for you will help me in my time of need. Help me, oh God, not to fear! Help me to trust in you! Help me to keep my eyes on Jesus, a sure foundation, a solid rock. Remind me of your promises. Bring to memory your Word. Surround me with your love, so that I can know your presence and be assured you are with me. Take this cup from me, Father, in heaven. And yet, I will praise your great name.*
>
> *In Jesus' name, Amen.*

Question to Consider

> *Consider the magnitude of how God, the creator of the universe, says he will uphold you and help you and that you shouldn't fear. What strength does the Lord offer you today in this knowledge?*

Day 2

Shock...and Awe

John 6:68

*Lord, to whom will we go? You have the words of
eternal life.*

It is a shocking experience to go abruptly from 100% a-ok
to feeling like you're at death's door. All in a single conversation with your doctor. The fear is palpable, but so can be the
presence of the Lord.

It had been a while (months...years?) since I had felt deeply
moved by the Holy Spirit leading up to my diagnosis. A friend
of mine even said I was a "functional atheist" despite being a
believer. Fortunately, despite my waywardness, God had been
faithful. Immediately after being diagnosed I was taken by the
Spirit to the hymn that goes, "On Christ the solid rock I stand,
all other ground is sinking sand, all other ground is sinking
sand." Such was the Lord's reminder to me in my deepest
moment of need.

Where do you turn during hard times? I hope it's to Christ.
That's really all there is when you think about it. Where does
the unbeliever usually turn? To YouTube videos, gurus, sur-
vivor groups, google searches for information, and to friends
and family. To counseling, therapy. To many things, even good
things to be sure, but none with a foundation so solid as the
Lord Jesus Christ.

In the early days of my diagnosis I was ceaselessly driven
to the Lord for comfort, and he met me mightily. That's not to
say it wasn't (and still isn't) hard. I shed many tears, but of
those tears, at least half of them have been out of joy for my
salvation in Christ. John 6:68 says, "Lord, to whom will we go?
You have the words of eternal life." Jesus had asked the discip-

les if they too were going to forsake him, but the truth is undeniable. Where else can we go when life falls apart? Jesus is the only sure foundation.

I was (and still am) shocked and saddened that they found a tumor in my esophagus. But I'm also in awe. God is so faithful.... In this most desperate hour, he is here. With me. With you. He loves us. No matter what, I know the worst thing that could ever happen to me would be to depart and be with Christ forever, worshiping Him, and that is not a bad thing to happen to anyone. Stand likewise in the firm foundation of the eternal life you have in Christ Jesus!

Prayer to the Lord

> *Lord Jesus, you are the solid rock on which I stand. All other ground is sinking sand. I praise you for being near me; draw near to me, oh Lord! I stand knocking at your door; open your door to me! I turn to you, Lord; come to me in power and in truth! You will sustain me through this deep valley. My flesh may fail, but your love for me never will.*
>
> *In Jesus' name, Amen.*

Question to Consider

> *If you know people who are strong believers in miracles, how can you connect further with them and be encouraged by their faith in the power of God?*

Day 3

A Way Maker

Luke 5:27-31

After these things He went out and saw a tax collector named Levi, sitting at the tax office. And He said to him, "Follow Me." So he left all, rose up, and followed Him.

Then Levi gave Him a great feast in his own house. And there were a great number of tax collectors and others who sat down with them. And their scribes and the Pharisees complained against His disciples, saying, "Why do you eat and drink with tax collectors and sinners?"

Jesus answered and said to them, "Those who are well have no need of a physician, but those who are sick."

In the past, I hardly ever listened to worship music at home. It's just not my "style" of music. That's changed now, however, likely for good. I've started listening to worship music non-stop.

But since I wasn't a frequent listener, I didn't have any "go-to" playlists for worship music. On the third day after my diagnosis, I simply asked Google to "play worship music" and the song "Way Maker" by Leeland immediately came up.

For me it was providence that this song came up first on the day I learned of my tumor. I was feeling very defeated, even morbid, like "I had received the sentence of death" (2 Corinthians 1:8-9). And yet, God reminded me of something in that critical moment, that he is a way maker, a miracle worker, a promise keeper, a light in the darkness, and that even when I cannot see it, he's working!

The song hit me like a ton of bricks, in a good way. It gave me hope for physical healing that I didn't have before. The C-word can feel hopeless, like a sentence of death, but God is a way maker; he can make a way through impossible odds. Believe it. Believe too in something that is possible only through faith—eternal life!

Anything is possible with God. He's a way maker, a promise keeper. No prognosis holds our fate. Jesus is not held hostage to the "odds" of survival. Do not trust the doctors or medicines, *per se*. Show them respect and honor, to be sure. However, put your trust in the Lord. After all, Jesus is "The Great Physician."

Way maker
Miracle worker
Promise keeper
Light in the darkness
My God, that is who you are

You are here
Touching every heart
I worship you
You are here
Healing every heart
I worship you
You are here
Turning lives around
I worship you
You are here
Mending every heart
I worship you

You wipe away all tears
You mend the broken heart
You're the answer to it all
Jesus

Prayer to the Lord

Lord Jesus, help me to believe in miracles. Help

me to put my hope in you, God, not statistics nor the odds. You are a way maker, a miracle worker, a promise keeper, oh Lord. Help me not to doubt you nor doubt your power to overcome the odds. You're the God of the universe! Give me hope, oh Lord. Give me peace, oh Lord. I ask you to heal me of cancer, in Jesus name! Grant me this mercy. Would the dust praise your name if I were to die (Psalms 30:9)? For your glory, and my joy, I pray for healing.

In Jesus' name, Amen.

Question to Consider

Leading to my question for you, I'd like to share a personal testimony.

Later that day when Google first played Way Maker, a friend from church texted my wife a prayer that my CT scan would be clear of metastasis. A few hours later I received the results of the CT scan and they had found no evidence of advanced metastasis. By all appearances, the cancer hadn't spread beyond some local lymph nodes!

And guess what.... Immediately after reading the results, Way Maker, by God's providence, played again on my playlist!

I saw this as an amazing revelation of God's love for me. That song came up twice in a single day at moments of desperate need and jubilant praise. Still today, it is a cornerstone in my playlist when I'm feeling depressed.

Do you recall a day or event where God revealed himself to you powerfully?

Day 4

Truth When Suffering Hits

2 Corinthians 1:8-9

*We do not want you to be unaware, brothers, of
the affliction we experienced in Asia..... We felt
that we had received the sentence of death. But
that was to make us rely not on ourselves but on
God who raises the dead.*

When we face trials of various kinds, we are learning to rely
not on ourselves, but on God.

Paul, too, felt he had received the sentence of death. He too
stared death in the face. He too had to turn away from self and
turn to God. It gives us hope to know that a man like Paul, an
apostle, a man filled with faith, still had to learn to turn to God
and rely on Him. This is obvious from the word "make", as his
affliction "made" him rely on God and not himself.

When I read this passage shortly after my diagnosis, it hit
all too close to home for me. For several years I'd been leaning
too heavily on my own understanding, contrary to what Proverbs 3:5 says. Or, as it relates to this verse, I'd been relying too
much on myself.

My health journey is a good example. I'd been hyper-
obsessed with losing weight and getting stronger in the gym.
Good goals to be sure, but they were mostly fueled by vanity
rather than a desire to steward my body well.

A year or so previous, my wife had said to me, "I haven't
seen you read your Bible in a while", and my response was that
for most of the past two thousand years nobody read their
Bibles (since most people were illiterate). But that only demonstrated how self-sufficient I had become. I didn't need to read
my Bible, I thought. Effectively, I didn't need God.

In our culture, it's understandable that we learn to lean so heavily on ourselves. Most YouTubers and other online influencers encourage self-sufficiency in the fight against cancer. A spirit of "you can do this!" and "you can beat cancer!" permeates self-help media. But when you first face the reality of cancer, when you feel that you have received the "sentence of death," no amount of self-help talk is of any value. It falls completely flat. It is completely void of power. You feel completely helpless.

But God! But in Christ Jesus there is power! For many, the day you get a cancer diagnosis is when you turn your face to Christ more than any other moment in life. Through it, you are being made to rely on God, because there literally is nothing else we *can* rely on that is certain. There is certainty found in Jesus and nowhere else.

So, is learning to rely on God a good thing? Yes. Is this cancer diagnosis therefore "a good and perfect gift" from God (James 1:17)? Yes.

This truth is sometimes hard to stomach. The fear is palpable. But you can know that God is doing a good work with you, for His glory and your joy.

I've often asked myself, when tempted by fear, *Would it be better to die one year from now, filled with the Holy Spirit, with a zeal for God and the gospel, fully relying on Him? Or would it be better to die 40 years from now but distant from God, fearful of death, clinging to life that is slipping away, uncertain of my salvation, uncertain of what comes after?*

Paul offers an answer: "To live is Christ, and to die is gain" (Philippians 1:21).

My hope is built on nothing less
Than Jesus' blood and righteousness;
I dare not trust the sweetest frame,
But wholly lean on Jesus' name.
On Christ, the solid Rock, I stand;
All other ground is sinking sand,
All other ground is sinking sand.

Prayer to the Lord

Lord Jesus, thank you for this tough lesson of cancer, for I am learning to rely on you like never before in my life. I repent, oh Lord, of my self-reliance in the past. I know now that anything in myself, and all other things, are unreliable as a source of hope. But you, Jesus, are the hope. You have met me in my hour of desperation and you have shown your face to me. Hallelujah! Praise God! Thank you, Jesus, for revealing yourself to me in my hour of need. Thank you even for cancer, because I will never be the same. I will forever keep my eyes on Jesus all the rest of my days and for all eternity. What a blessing to know the Lord! What a comfort! Cancer, oh Jesus, is a gift...and a great evil to be sure, but you are using it for good, Lord. Thank you for turning this evil thing toward my good and your glory, Jesus, and not toward my destruction. I commit the rest of my life to you, Jesus, to seeking your face, to worshiping you in spirit and in truth. By your grace I will never go back to my former ways. Thank you. I love you. Thank you for first loving me.

In Jesus' name, Amen.

Question to Consider

At times, God uses the "megaphone of suffering" to speak into our hearts (see The Problem of Pain *by C.S. Lewis). In what ways may God be using cancer to break through your hardness of heart and draw you closer to himself?*

Day 5

An Astonishing Hope

2 Corinthians 4:17

This light momentary affliction is preparing for us an eternal weight of glory beyond all comparison.

A dear brother from many years ago sent me an audio clip by Tim Keller. Tim eventually died of cancer after fighting it multiple times over 20+ years.

The clip was posted with the article "Death Can Only Make Me Better: Remembering Tim Keller" at DesiringGod.org, and here is a key quote from it that really encouraged me:

> If Jesus Christ really died on the cross, taking our punishment, and he's now raised from the dead, now when we believe in him, not only are our sins forgiven, but now we have an incredible hope about the future. We're going to be raised, and everything in this world is going to be put right, and there is not going to be any suffering or death. *That is an astonishing hope.*

This reminded me of 2 Corinthians 4:17, where Paul describes his imprisonment and likely death as "light" in comparison to the astonishing hope he has in Christ Jesus!

Light!

And yet it's so true.

The hope we have in Christ Jesus *is* astonishing. When all other hopes fall down, God is here with you, right now, pointing you to Jesus.

I know if you can keep your eyes fixed on Jesus, you can endure anything. You can come through it, you can have true courage, because the worst thing that can happen to you is the attainment of infinite joy, a perfect body, and—best of all—a new life in the presence of Jesus that lasts forever. What you have to look forward to is nothing short of an "eternal weight of glory beyond all comparison."

What an astonishing hope! Death, where is your sting?!

Prayer to the Lord

Father God, thank you for loving me so much that you sent your Son to die for me, that I may have confidence in everlasting life, no matter the outcome of this cancer. Thank you for this great hope, this assurance. Without it I would despair utterly. But by your grace, Father, I can stand. I can hope. Hope for healing to be sure, but moreover, hope for everlasting life! By the power of the name of Jesus, death has no hold over me.

In Jesus' name, Amen!

Question to Consider

How is affliction preparing you for glory today?

Day 6

For the Joy Set Before Him

Hebrews 12:1–3, NIV

Let us run with perseverance the race marked out for us, fixing our eyes on Jesus, the pioneer and perfecter of our faith. For the joy set before him he endured the cross, scorning its shame, and sat down at the right hand of the throne of God. Consider him who endured such opposition from sinners, so that you will not grow weary and lose heart.

Today's meditation is a paraphrase of the sermon by Tim Keller that I quoted from in yesterday's entry. It impacted me mightily, for we see, in the words from Hebrews, the courage that Jesus had in the face of death on a cross. How was he able to endure it? From where did He get his courage? How should we think about courage in times like this? Tim says:

> The first part of courage is looking away from yourself. The world tells you, "Look at yourself and banish fear." The second part of courage is looking toward hope, getting hope. Real courage is not the absence of fear; it's the presence of joy....
>
> I actually think the garden of Gethsemane is the place where you see the greatest act of courage in the history of the world, because by the time [Jesus] got nailed to the cross, even if he wanted to turn around, it would have been too late. There he was, nailed to the cross. But that night [in the Garden of Gethsemane], he could have left. In fact, he even thought about it. He says, "My soul is overwhelmed...to the point of death"

(Matthew 26:38, NIV). What do you see in Jesus Christ? You see courage.

You don't see him saying, "Bring it on." The bloody sweat showed he was feeling fear. He wasn't saying, "Come on." What was he doing? We're told all about it in Hebrews 12:1–3:

> Let us run with perseverance the race marked out for us, fixing our eyes on Jesus, the pioneer and perfecter of our faith. For the joy set before him he endured the cross, scorning its shame, and sat down at the right hand of the throne of God. Consider him who endured such opposition from sinners, so that you will not grow weary and lose heart.
> Hebrews 12:1–3 (NIV)

There it is. He looked away from himself, and what did he look toward? Joy. What was the joy? The joy of pleasing his Father and redeeming his friends. The joy of that enabled him to have courage. Listen: if you see him courageously dying for you like that so you can say to death, "Spare not, do thy worst," then you can have courage.

Where does our courage come from? Our courage is rooted in our joy in God, the joy of our salvation, the joy of doing the will of our Father in heaven. True courage like this pushes down fear.

When you turn your eyes toward Jesus, the fear abates. When you turn your eyes away from Jesus, the fear rises up again. Alas, such is the rollercoaster we call cancer!

But the sweet grace of Jesus in this awful battle is that you're learning, desperately, to turn to Jesus continuously, all day, every day, for courage in the face of cancer.

It was for the joy set before Him that Jesus endured the cross, and it would be wise to give much consideration to him. In considering Jesus, thinking and meditating on Him, you will not grow weary and lose heart. All other ground is sinking sand. Nothing else pushes down the fear more than your hope in Jesus and the knowledge of God's love for you. And, because of the joy set before you, you too can endure anything.

Prayer to the Lord

Lord Jesus, may I hope in you for my courage. May I not look into myself, may I not attempt to muster up the willpower of courage, for my willpower is no sure thing. It will fail me. But you, Jesus, will never leave me, you will never forsake me! May I truly believe that death has lost its sting (1 Corinthians 15:55-57) because of the hope set before me in Christ Jesus. From that hope fear has no dominion over me. From this hope I am given a spirit not of fear, but of power, love, and sound judgment (2 Timothy 1:7)!

In Jesus' name, Amen.

Question to Consider

What is at the root of your courage in the face of cancer? Is your courage rooted in yourself, an internet influencer/guru, your doctors, or in God? Do you agree with Tim that true courage is not the absence of fear but the presence of joy? What does that mean for you personally?

Day 7

Appointed for Salvation

1 Thessalonians 5:9-10

For God did not appoint us to wrath, but to obtain salvation through our Lord Jesus Christ, who died for us, so that whether we are awake or asleep, we may live together with him.

(The following journal entry was written on the 7th day of having received news of my tumor. I left it in its original form to leave it as a testimony of God's power in us when we seek him. To God be the glory.)

It's been the hardest week of my life, and yet God is still good. Today is my first oncology consultation appointment. Today, I start my healing journey. I'm thankful and eager to get started!

But the peace of God that overwhelms me in this moment is because I know that, no matter what, I will be forever with Jesus. I will be with Jesus in life. I will be alive with Jesus even if this body of mine perishes. Praise be to God in Christ Jesus for his assurances of salvation!

As I set out, eager to pursue healing and to start treatment, I put my hope not in being healed, but in the power of God and the knowledge that nothing bad can happen to me. Death can only make me stronger!

Prayer to the Lord

Lord Jesus, I pray by the power of your Holy Name that you would heal me of cancer. I pray you would provide the doctors with divine wisdom in the recommended course of treatment. I pray the treatment will be effective and lasting. I also pray against Satan, who is always prowling, looking for opportunities to tempt me to fear. I pray against him in Jesus' name! I pray you would strengthen me in the only ways you can, in giving me an eternal hope and a strong confidence that you, Jesus, are indeed the Great Physician! There is nothing you are not capable of. Your name, oh Jesus, is greater than cancer! You hold the universe in the palm of your hand! I praise your name, Father God. Thank you for walking with me!

In Jesus' name, Amen.

Question to Consider

Which do you ponder more...your cancer, or your hope for salvation and eternal life?

Day 8

The Things that are Unseen

2 Corinthians 4:17-18

This light momentary affliction is preparing for us an eternal weight of glory beyond all comparison, as we look not to the things that are seen but to the things that are unseen. For the things that are seen are transient, but the things that are unseen are eternal.

I wrote this journal entry on a day I did not feel like writing. Later that day I was scheduled for an ultrasound and would find out what stage my cancer was. It felt like a heavy day. But every day had been heavy and I just needed to keep looking toward Jesus for my strength, keep praying to Him, keep worshiping Him, keep being encouraged by His church. It's a *fight* for faith!

It's days like that where Paul's words in 2 Corinthians 4:17-18 can really help us. The fear I felt at that time was unlike anything I'd ever felt in my entire life. And yet, Paul says even that deep concern for my health is incomparable to the weight of glory being prepared for us. What feels so heavy now is offset by the knowledge that no matter what, this affliction is indeed momentary. Something is coming that is eternal, forever, that will *never* fail—a weight of glory.

Why is "a weight of glory" being prepared for us? What does that mean? Whose glory? God's glory, to be sure, but I also think Paul here is talking about our glorified bodies when we arrive in heaven. A perfect body with no disease, with no sadness or fear, is truly glorious thing to obtain.

The physical things that are seen are transient, temporary. Our bodies will give way to death eventually. It's inevitable. But the things that are unseen are eternal! Our spirit and soul are eternal. If we die, we will not die! When our body dies, within one millisecond we will be taken up and be with Christ.

I know this because Jesus told the repentant criminal on the cross, "Today you will be with me in paradise" (Luke 23:43). *Today.* Not tomorrow, not 3,000 years from then or whenever Jesus comes back. Today. Our soul, the thing unseen, is eternal. We will live forever, in Jesus' name! Amen.

Prayer to the Lord

Lord Jesus, help me not to center myself on this affliction of cancer. Rather, help me to center myself on the hope I have in Christ Jesus. Cancer, oh Lord, is momentary. But you, oh Lord, are eternal! And I have life in you forever! My tumor is a momentary affliction that is seen, but you, through faith, are manifest to me as an eternal weight of glory that makes my cancer seem tiny and insignificant by comparison. My hope for salvation and a new body is a weight of glory incomprehensible. However, for some reason at this moment I also still feel the fear. Push it down, oh Lord, and give me the peace of God that only you can supply! I walk not in my strength, oh Lord, for I have none. I walk in the strength of the Lord and his Holy Spirit.

In Jesus' name, Amen.

Question to Consider

How can you build routine into your days to ensure you are consistently creating space and time to look at the things that are unseen?

Day 9

Wait for the Lord

Psalms 33, 46, and 27

We wait for the LORD;
he is our help and shield.
For our hearts rejoice in him
because we trust in his holy name.
May your faithful love rest on us, LORD,
for we put our hope in you.
                    (Psalm 33:20-22)

He says, "Be still, and know that I am God;
I will be exalted among the nations,
I will be exalted in the earth."
                    (Psalm 46:10)

Wait for the LORD;
be strong, and let your heart be courageous.
Wait for the LORD.
                    (Psalm 27:14)

I've learned that one of the hardest things about walking with cancer is the waiting.

Fear pops up, but the promises of God push it down. But the waiting...the waiting is unavoidable and distressing.

You have great hope in getting in to see a doctor, but then they tell you it will be three weeks before you can get in to see him or her. Or, you have great hope for some good news with an upcoming test, but then the doctor tells you it'll be a week or so before you get the results.

Cancer makes time slow down. At one point I was remarking to my wife how fast it seemed that summer was just flying by. But then, just a few weeks later, it seemed as if summer was just crawling by at a glacial pace. You feel the weight of every day, every hour, even every minute. The waiting is exhausting, draining, depleting. The waiting is a heavy burden.

How do we wait well, with courage, hope, and even joy?

These verses in Psalms have encouraged me to wait well, to "wait on the Lord" instead of waiting on doctors and test results. David tells us some awesome things about waiting for the Lord. We wait for the Lord, instead of test results, because:

- He is our help and shield (verse 20)
- Our hearts rejoice in him (verse 21)
- We can trust him (verse 21)
- His love rests on us (verse 22)
- Our hope is in him (verse 22)

It's so easy to see doctors as our help and shield (and to a degree they are). It's so easy to rejoice in good news from a particular test result (and we should). It's so easy to trust in the odds of survival (when the odds are good, that is). It's so easy to put our hope in a test result or surgical procedure (you just want it *out!*). However, none of these things make the waiting any easier. Unknowns remain, and time passes at a grueling pace.

Psalms 46:10 tells us why waiting for the Lord is always the better, surer alternative:

"Be still, and know that I am God."

We should wait on the Lord precisely because he is God...

- He is our help and shield, because he is God.
- Our hearts rejoice in Him, because he is God.
- We can trust in Him, because he is God.
- His love rests on us, because he is God and sent his Son to die for us.
- Our hope is in him, because he is God.

God has the universe in the palm of his glorious, all-powerful, all majestic hands; our cancer is in his hands too; this sovereignty is a part of the very definition of who God is. This knowledge of God being none other than *God* is what makes the waiting manageable.

Why? Because there's no uncertainty in it. The odds are 100% that God is...God!

The truth of the coming revelation of the glory of Jesus is certain. The truth that God loves us is already proven (he sent his Son to die for us—John 3:16). The proof that there's power in the name of Jesus to heal is already demonstrated through the healings in the gospels and the multitude of people who witnessed and bore witness to them.

We have a surer foundation to wait on than doctor's' visits and test results. Anxiety still lingers in those things when we wait on them. But when we wait on the Lord our feet are on solid ground. Minute by minute we can sing his praises and the anxiety of waiting is pushed down. The presence of the Lord makes waiting bearable.

Therefore, with all hope and expectation, this is my paraphrase of those Psalms, my prayer from them:

Prayer to the Lord

> *I will wait for you, LORD;*
> *being strong, and letting my heart be courageous,*
> *waiting for you, LORD,*
> *For you are my help and my shield.*
> *My heart rejoices in you,*
> *because I trust in your holy name.*
> *May your faithful love rest on me, LORD,*
> *for I put my hope in you.*
> *My heart is at peace, knowing you are God.*
> *You will be exalted in my waiting;*
> *you will be exalted in my cancer.*

> *In Jesus name, Amen.*

Question to Consider

Why is being "still" a key element of knowing God is God? Are you finding time to "be still" in your daily routine?

Day 10

We're Given a Spirit...

2 Timothy 1:7

God has not given us a spirit of fear, but one of power, love, and sound judgment.

The Holy Spirit of God dwells within us. What effect does this indwelling of the Spirit of God have on us? One effect is the conquering of our fear, and he does this by replacing it with power, love, and sound judgment. Let's take a closer look at each of these blessings.

A spirit of power

Fear and powerlessness go hand in hand. I think this is why cancer is so scary; you can really feel powerless against cancer. It's interesting therefore that Paul mentions a spirit of power, because if we have power, we have control. Power for what, and control over what?

Paul says we're given a "spirit" of power, so we can safely assume that is a power over spiritual things. We're given power over spiritual forces of darkness that tempt us to fear and lose hope. We're given power over our own sin and unbelief because God is good and has a good plan for us.

However, this power also spills into physical things too. Jesus, by the power of his command, healed many while he lived on the earth. Then he sent his Holy Spirit so that his powerful presence would dwell within us.

It's a mystery to me, but Jesus says that even a tiny bit of faith would allow us to move mountains (Matthew 17:20). Therefore, I believe the Spirit of God within us has power over physical things too, such as healing our bodies.

However, the Spirit of God isn't ours to command, *per se*; God is still God and his will must come to pass. We pray to God knowing that we can only be healed by his sovereign will and power. And even if healing is not his plan for us at this time, we still have a fear-killing spirit of power that comes from knowing that "all things work together for the good" (Romans 8:28).

We are not helpless or powerless over fear and cancer. Quite the opposite really; the power of God within us can well up into a peace that surpasses understanding (Philippians 4:7). Peace in all circumstances is an amazing gift of power, and we should pray for it and praise God when we receive it.

A spirit of love

Jesus commanded us to love one another, and he also boiled down the whole Old Testament to loving God and our neighbor, which he said were the two greatest commandments (Matthew 22:34-40).

But he doesn't just command us, he also gives us what we need to obey; namely, a spirit of love. God supplies what we need. You don't have a spirit of fear, but rather one of love within you.

Jesus said the world will know we are his disciples because they will see our love for others (John 13:35). God grants this spirit of love to all those who believe in Christ. Some may receive the spirit in different measures, some more, some less, but all have it who are in Christ Jesus.

Walk therefore in love for others, not fear for oneself.

A spirit of sound judgment

Our spiritual lives are often marked by strong emotions. In worship, for example, believers often raise their hands, cry out to God, or even shed tears as they joyfully praise God.

However, rational thinking is also an important part of our spiritual lives. We don't believe blindly as unbelievers may suggest. Rather, we believe with the full capacities of our mind, where we contemplate the experiences of God in our lives, the promises of God in his Word, and the historical work of God through the ages.

When we meditate on these things with the sound judgment God has given us, we are empowered to war against fear. We have objective truths on which we can stand in the midst of something even as terrible as cancer. Sometimes when fear rises up, using your sound judgment is the best way to fight. For example, you can consider the following in your mind and be strengthened:

- God, the creator of the universe, loves you (Romans 8:35, 37-39)
- God has a good plan for you, and he will carry you (Philippians 1:6)
- God has saved you, and will save you, from all your sins (John 3:16)
- God will give you a new, perfect, and glorified physical body (Philippians 3:20-4:1)
- Even if you die, you know you will never die (John 11:25-26)
- There is power in the name of Jesus to heal (Acts 3:16)

Dwell on the truths and promises of God and be strengthened against all fear.

Prayer to the Lord

> *Father God, thank you for giving me your Holy Spirit to live in my heart, to strengthen and encourage me through all circumstances. Thank you that your Spirit gives me power over fear. Thank you for helping me to love. Thank you for your promises, oh Lord. Help me to meditate on them daily. Thank you for fighting against the fear I feel. I pray fear would give way to joy, joy in knowing you, joy in knowing your love for me, and joy knowing your promises for me.*
>
> *In Jesus' name, Amen.*

Question to Consider

When fear starts to rise up within you, what promises of God encourage you the most?

Day 11

Bread From Heaven

John 6:35, 57-58

"I am the bread of life," Jesus told them. "No one who comes to me will ever be hungry, and no one who believes in me will ever be thirsty again....

"Just as the living Father sent me and I live because of the Father, so the one who feeds on me will live because of me. This is the bread that came down from heaven; it is not like the manna your ancestors ate—and they died. The one who eats this bread will live forever."

Jesus is how we endure cancer. Jesus is our promise for healing. Jesus is our confidence in the face of fear of dying, for we know that those who are in him will never taste death.

In the story of manna from heaven, God foreshadowed his defeat of death over a thousand years before Jesus came to earth. Indeed, stories like this, when the Bible is understood end-to-end, paint a tapestry of God's good purposes throughout history—it's all pointing to Jesus, including the history of our lives.

Physical bread vs. spiritual bread

It's important here to understand the context for Jesus' metaphor of hunger, thirst, and "feeding on me."

After God delivered Israel out of Egypt, they wandered in the Sinai wilderness for 40 years. Not long into that wandering, they ran out of food and were starving. The Israelites lamented to God that God delivered them out of Egypt simply to have them die of starvation in the desert (Exodus 16:3). But

God heard their cries and he sent manna from heaven, an unleavened bread-like substance that appeared each morning with the dew.

In John 6 Jesus tells us that the manna in heaven was a foreshadowing of God's ultimate provision of "bread" in Christ Jesus. However, the "bread" of Jesus leads to eternal life, whereas the bread from the manna only sustained the physical body for a day or so and they became hungry again.

The point of both stories is that God provides sustenance to his people leading to life. On the one hand, God does provide for our physical life here on earth, but that provision is temporary, just like the manna was temporary.

We will eventually die, whether one year from now or 40. But God tells us we will *never* die, because Jesus is the bread of life—life eternal!

Spiritual and emotional satisfaction is found in Christ

Jesus tells us that if we come to him, we will never be hungry or thirsty again. This metaphor speaks to our spiritual and emotional contentment. We can be in the wilderness of cancer and yet be full of life, purpose, and hope in Christ Jesus.

Though it's a dark valley, when cancer causes us to turn our face to Jesus and seek his presence, we are told Jesus will fill our bellies, so to speak. Jesus will be near to us; he will comfort us. The fear the Israelites felt at their lack of food and impending starvation will not be a fear we share, because Jesus will replace that fear with faith and trust in him.

As cancer sufferers, we cry out to God for a longer life. The Israelites in the wilderness cried out to God because they were starving, and God supplied bread so that they wouldn't die. Likewise, the Father has supplied bread to us so that we will *never* die.

Metaphorically, if we feast on Jesus, if we saturate our lives with Jesus, if we pursue him and keep our eyes fixed on him, we indeed will never die.

This is the bread of life: Jesus. Eat of this bread every day and you'll always be satisfied.

Prayer to the Lord

Lord Jesus, help me to come to you when I am afraid, for I know in you I will find contentment and satisfaction. Thank you for allowing your body to be killed so that I may attain a perfect body through the power of your resurrection. While I wait for this great gift, thank you for the gift of your Holy Spirit so that I would never be hungry or thirsty even in this broken body of mine. Help me to keep my eyes on you.

In Jesus' name, Amen.

Question to Consider

What kind of "manna" are you consuming each day in an attempt to find satisfaction? Could some of your daily activities be replaced or supplemented with more feasting on Jesus?

Day 12

Hear My Pleas for Mercy

Psalm 28:1–2, 6-7

Lord, I call to you;
my rock, do not be deaf to me.
If you remain silent to me,
I will be like those going down to the Pit.
Listen to the sound of my pleading
when I cry to you for help,
when I lift up my hands
toward your holy sanctuary....
Blessed be the Lord,
for he has heard the sound of my pleading.
The Lord is my strength and my shield;
my heart trusts in him, and I am helped.
Therefore my heart celebrates,
and I give thanks to him with my song.

Isaiah 38:1-5

In those days Hezekiah became terminally ill.
The prophet Isaiah son of Amoz came and said
to him, "This is what the Lord says: 'Set your
house in order, for you are about to die; you will
not recover.'"

Then Hezekiah turned his face to the wall
and prayed to the Lord. He said, "Please, Lord,
remember how I have walked before you faith-
fully and wholeheartedly, and have done what
pleases you." And Hezekiah wept bitterly.

Then the word of the Lord came to Isaiah:
"Go and tell Hezekiah, 'This is what the Lord
God of your ancestor David says: I have heard

*your prayer; I have seen your tears. Look, I am
going to add fifteen years to your life.'"*

We see two kings of Israel in these passages crying out to the Lord. David, in the Psalm, cries out to God, his "solid rock". He asks God not to be "deaf toward me" and prays earnestly for God to "hear my pleas for mercy."

Likewise, Hezekiah "wept bitterly" because of his terminal illness, praying for healing. Amazingly, God hears Hezekiah's prayer. God saw his tears and responded by mercifully granting Hezekiah 15 more years of life.

We can learn a lot from several things these two kings had in common...

David and Hezekiah were deeply saddened

You can feel the power of their emotions in these verses. David pleads and cries to the Lord for help. Hezekiah weeps bitterly. It should encourage us to see such men, kings no less, so dependent upon the Lord yet still in touch with their emotions. They were not in the habit of pushing down and burying their feelings. Instead, they brought their cries to the Lord, and the Lord heard their cries for help. The opposite of this, which is popular in some cancer communities and groups, is to "man up to cancer" and other calls to be boss over our diagnoses. But we shouldn't look to ourselves for the strength to face cancer, but rather we should look to God for strength and bring to him all our fears and sadness and cries for help.

They put their hope in God for mercy and healing

At the end of the day, the Lord is our only solid rock on which we can stand, and on which David and Hezekiah stood. Our willpower is not a solid rock from which to fight cancer, but the Lord is a sure foundation, our strength, our shield. David and Hezekiah called to the Lord in their hour of desperate need, for mercy on one hand and healing on the other.

This is yet another reminder about the source of our hope.

We trust our doctors, but we put our hope in the Lord.

We cry out for mercy and healing knowing that we *will* be granted it, either in the here and now or certainly in eternity. We cry out to God with an astonishing hope and expectation of victory in the Lord. Even as kings, sovereign over the land and people, they still wept bitterly at their lack of actual control and went instead to the One who reigned supreme with ultimate control over all things and all circumstances.

Their response is thankfulness and praise

Having been granted mercy and healing, our only appropriate response is to praise God. We have been granted forgiveness and acceptance in Christ Jesus...all our sins are covered, gone forever, by God's grace toward us.

We have been granted new bodies in Christ Jesus as well, and we will surely be given that which is promised.

These truths are the solid rock of astonishing hope on which we stand in the face of any difficult circumstances, not the least of which is cancer. We *will* defeat cancer, and we should rejoice in the promises of God for us and for all who are in Christ Jesus.

Prayer to the Lord

> *Father God, you are my refuge, my strong tower, my hope. Hear my cries for mercy, oh Lord, and my cries for healing, my mighty God. For in you there is power to forgive sins and to heal. Thank you for forgiving me. Thank you for the promise I have of eternal life. Grant me many more years, oh Lord, as you granted Hezekiah, to sing your praises and glorify your name through my life, I pray. And yet, not as I will, oh Lord, but as you will. To you be the glory, forever.*
>
> *In Jesus' name, Amen.*

Question to Consider

When your emotions run high, is your first inclination to bring them to the Lord, or to suppress and run from them (perhaps through entertainment or other distractions)?

Day 13

We are Immensely Valuable to the Lord

Matthew 10:29-31

Aren't two sparrows sold for a penny? Yet not one of them falls to the ground without your Father's consent. But even the hairs of your head have all been counted. So don't be afraid; you are worth more than many sparrows.

What kind of God do we believe in? A god who passively watches the events of the world unfold, or a God who is active personally in our lives? This verse answers that question definitively.

Not only is God actively involved in our lives, but he also supremely governs all of creation, down to the last breath an individual sparrow takes.

God didn't cause our cancer, *per se*. Cancer is a great evil that is caused by the brokenness of a fallen, sinful world. Because of sin, the Bible says, all things are subject to futility, including our bodies (Romans 8:20). But that is not the end of God's involvement. He didn't cause our cancer, but he did choose to allow it.

At first we may recoil at this. How can God allow something so evil to happen to us? How can even a single sparrow dying be a part of his sovereign plan? He permits evil to happen, while not causing it, because he knows he can use it for our good. Satan may have given us cancer, but not without God's permission first (see the story of Job in the Bible).

While we may initially recoil, this fact of God's sovereign plan for our lives inevitably gives way to a profound peace; our cancer is not in vain. It is not meaningless. God, the creator of the universe, is at work in our lives for our good (Romans 8:28).

We also see the undeniable love of God for us in this verse. We see our value in the comparison to a sparrow dying, and even more when we realize that Jesus suffered death himself on a cross so that we could be resurrected with him and have eternal life!

God didn't just throw up his hands when creation fell into sin. Instead, because of his love for us, he sent his Son to redeem us from this fallen world.

How then can we be afraid? We have a God who loves us more than we can even imagine, and this very same God has a plan for us—a plan to take this evil in our life and turn it for our good (see the testimony of Joseph in Genesis 50:20). If a sparrow cannot breathe its last breath without God's permission, cancer never happens without God knowing how he plans to use it to bring us joyfully closer to him in the end.

Trust, therefore, in the love of God for you. Know that our God is not aloof, casually being entertained by the happenings of the world. Instead, he is actively engaged in your life personally, intimately. Jesus didn't come to die for the sake of sparrows, but he did die for you. You are infinitely more valuable than all the birds in the world when you consider that the creator of the universe gave his life for you.

Prayer to the Lord

Father in heaven, I glorify the name of Jesus. Thank you, Father, for loving me so much that you sent your Son to die for me. You turned the sin of Adam around; evil had befallen the world, but you are still at work in this world for our good through Christ Jesus. Thank you, too, for how you're turning this suffering I'm enduring around for my good. Your plans for me are not done. My joy is not yet full. Draw me nearer to you every day so that I can rejoice in suffering and bring glory to your name through my songs of praise. May others see your love for them just as you have shown me your love for me. May I tell everyone of your love for them in Christ. Help me to be at peace even while I have cancer, so that they would see the peace of God in my life and be drawn toward Jesus.

In Jesus' name, Amen.

Question to Consider

How is God's plan for your life becoming more apparent now that you (or your loved one) has cancer?

Day 14

The Good Shepherd

Psalm 23

The Lord is my shepherd;
I have what I need.
He lets me lie down in green pastures;
he leads me beside quiet waters.
He renews my life;
he leads me along the right paths
for his name's sake.
Even when I go through the darkest valley,
I fear no danger,
for you are with me;
your rod and your staff—they comfort me.
You prepare a table before me
in the presence of my enemies;
you anoint my head with oil;
my cup overflows.
Only goodness and faithful love will pursue me
all the days of my life,
and I will dwell in the house of the Lord
as long as I live.

This psalm, often referred to as The Good Shepherd, is written by David and often sung as a praise song to God. There's a lot of encouragement for the sufferer in this psalm, so let's look carefully at each part.

"The Lord is my shepherd; I have what I need"

David sees the Lord as his Shepherd, which means he sees the Lord as his protector, provider, and guide. The Lord protects his life, which is how his "cup overflows" despite being in the presence of his enemies; they are no match for the power of his Shepherd.

Like sheep who have a good shepherd, David has been provided everything he needs—namely the Shepherd himself. David needs food, housing, clothes and many things, but the context here suggests that what he needs most of all is the presence of his Shepherd. We too, in our suffering, need the Lord more than anything, and he gives himself to us abundantly when we seek him.

"He renews my life; he leads me along the right paths for his name's sake"

The Lord renews life in David, which I take to mean that he delivers David from desperation.

When you read the psalms of David, you see a continuous stream of crying out to the Lord in desperation and sadness, followed by David praising God for his deliverance or anticipated future deliverance. You see this oscillation between desperation and praise, a continual renewing of life in David's spirit through faith in God's grace toward him.

This is the "right path" David is led on, the path of continual dependency on the Lord. Sheep, after all, are continually dependent upon the protection and provision of their shepherd.

Amazingly, David doesn't assume the goodness of God is for his own sake, despite receiving an abundance of joy and comfort. However, his needs and desires are secondary to the glory due to the name of the Lord Jesus. Jesus' name is worthy of praise because of how he leads us and renews the life within us despite the challenging circumstances we face. We get the joy, but Jesus gets the glory for doing the work.

"Even when I go through the darkest valley, I fear no danger, for you are with me; your rod and your staff—they comfort me"

David was continually under pressure for his throne from even his own sons, who rebelled against him, and yet he says he fears no danger. This is because his great Shepherd is with him, and the presence of his Shepherd comforts him despite the danger all around him.

We too can know this peace of God even in the midst of cancer. Cancer may be a deep, dark valley, but if we stay close to Jesus, fear will have no dominion over us. The guiding and protecting presence of Jesus will be a powerful comfort to us.

"You prepare a table before me in the presence of my enemies; you anoint my head with oil; my cup overflows"

David's cup overflows with provision and joy despite the continuous presence of enemies all around him. David has not been overcome. David has overcome his enemies through the presence of his powerful Shepherd, the Lord. We likewise *will* overcome cancer. It is our certain expectation. Cancer is a weak and feeble enemy compared to the power of our great Shepherd, Jesus. When we trust in him, our cup will overflow with confidence in him.

"Only goodness and faithful love will pursue me all the days of my life, and I will dwell in the house of the Lord as long as I live"

This is the power of our Shepherd, the Lord Jesus. Despite the darkest valley we've ever walked in, Jesus grants us faithful love and mercy. He not only grants it, but faithful love and mercy pursue us! The love of God pursues us all our life; great is the faithfulness of our Lord!

Our bodies are the temple of the Spirit of God (1 Corinthians 6:19-20). God dwells within us! We will dwell with God in his house all the days of our life, and then when we die physically, we will learn that in fact we never can die. We will immediately dwell with Jesus spiritually until our soul is joined to our made-new, perfect bodies, at Jesus' return to this earth. In this way we never die, even if our bodies temporarily pass away.

Praise be to God for this astounding hope we have in Christ Jesus!

Prayer to the Lord

Lord Jesus, thank you for protecting me, for providing all I need, and for guiding me along the right paths, all my life. I give you the glory, oh Lord, because I know there's no way I could walk through this dark valley without you. I would succumb to fear, my heart would melt. But your presence strengthens me. You renew my life and my joy in knowing you and your salvation. Praise be to God for my deliverance!

In Jesus' name, Amen.

Question to Consider

Do you think that you have what you need to fight this battle of cancer? If not, seek first the Kingdom of God and know that "all these things will be provided for you" (Matthew 6:33).

Day 15

Keep Your Eyes on Jesus

Matthew 14:22-33

Immediately he made the disciples get into the boat and go ahead of him to the other side, while he dismissed the crowds. After dismissing the crowds, he went up on the mountain by himself to pray. Well into the night, he was there alone. Meanwhile, the boat was already some distance from land, battered by the waves, because the wind was against them. Jesus came toward them walking on the sea very early in the morning. When the disciples saw him walking on the sea, they were terrified. "It's a ghost!" they said, and they cried out in fear.

Immediately Jesus spoke to them. "Have courage! It is I. Don't be afraid."

"Lord, if it's you," Peter answered him, "command me to come to you on the water."

He said, "Come."

And climbing out of the boat, Peter started walking on the water and came toward Jesus. But when he saw the strength of the wind, he was afraid, and beginning to sink he cried out, "Lord, save me!"

Immediately Jesus reached out his hand, caught hold of him, and said to him, "You of little faith, why did you doubt?"

When they got into the boat, the wind ceased. Then those in the boat worshiped him and said, "Truly you are the Son of God."

This story of Peter walking on water is a great picture of what it looks like to walk in faith in the midst of a storm—even when you're not perfect. Peter had faith and came out onto the water, but then doubt overcame him and caused him to fear. And yet the Lord comforted Peter and restored him.

Five features of this story provide instruction and encouragement for those of us who are ravaged by the winds and waves of cancer:

Peter wanted a sign

I think it's interesting that when Peter saw the Lord, he said, "Lord, if it's you," and he wanted a sign that would prove he was indeed the Lord. This encourages me because it normalizes doubt. We all want to believe and trust in Christ completely, but doubts inevitably creep in. Peter himself, "the rock" on which the church was built, had doubts despite seeing a miracle right before his eyes.

It's also interesting that Peter put God to the test. Peter took his doubt and put it before the Lord, saying, "If it's you, command me to come to you on the water." I think there are two things we can learn from this.

First, his doubt led to productive action; he actively pursued answers rather than simply doubting and then walking away from the faith, which so many do. Doubt should cause us to pursue answers from the Lord, not walk away from him!

Second, in a way Peter was testing Jesus by asking him to command him to come out on the deadly waters, and it didn't end well for Peter. The other men in the boat were content to believe without needing to test the Lord, and I suggest that should be our usual approach as well. Jesus himself discouraged putting God to the test when he himself was tempted by the devil to do just that (Luke 4:12). So ask God to give you the blessing of believing without seeing (John 20:29).

Peter had his eyes on Jesus when he walked on the water

Regardless of whether it was wise of Peter to ask for the command from Jesus, he is to be commended for obeying it. His faith in that initial obedience produced a second miracle, Peter's own walking on water. The point here is that God will do amazing things in our lives if we listen to his voice, if we obey what he tells us to do.

When called, Peter didn't stay on the boat; he stepped out, and the glory of God was revealed through his faith and obedience. Likewise, we should get out of the proverbial boat when Jesus commands us to!

Peter began to fear when he took his eyes off Jesus

Even after his notable act of faith and obedience, Peter wasn't without his doubts. When Peter saw the wind and the waves, even he began to fear.

For me, this is all too poignant. I know from my own journey with cancer that if I take my eyes off Jesus for even a second, fear wells up within me. Like Peter, we cancer sufferers are confident and comforted when we look to Jesus, but when we look away to our circumstances we become fearful or depressed.

For me, "looking away" takes the form of trusting in doctors more than trusting in God, fretting over an upcoming PET scan, or pouring myself into Netflix and video games to bury my feelings, which only works for so long before they come roaring back even worse than before.

Such feelings are normal, however, and we shouldn't forget that Peter cried out to the Lord in response to his fear. He didn't suppress his fear by trying to ignore it; he cried out. It's always better to cry out to the Lord for strength than to pretend you have no fear or sadness.

When Peter cried out to Jesus, Jesus immediately drew near to him and took hold of him

I will *never* forget the initial shock and fear of receiving my cancer diagnosis. But I also will *never* forget the nearness of God's Holy Spirit in that moment of my utmost despair. I cried out to the Lord, and the Lord "reached out his hand" and "caught hold" of me. What an amazing God we have!

And yet that is only the first part of this striking verse. Jesus said to Peter, "You of little faith, why did you doubt?" In our fear and doubt, God draws near and comforts us, yes, but he also commends us to greater faith in him.

In hindsight, I believe that if my faith had been stronger when I received my diagnosis, I wouldn't have felt so much fear and despair. I believe that if we keep our eyes on Jesus, we can walk on the proverbial waters despite the raging waves and wind, never sinking. Peter could have done that, and we can too.

My point here isn't that I'm beating myself up for the fear and despair I felt in those early days of being diagnosed (and still do at times, to be honest). Rather I want to encourage you to pray like I do for myself. I pray earnestly that the Lord would strengthen my faith, so that fear would have no dominion over me.

On the day before my very first treatment of Chemo/Radiation, I wrote this in my journal: "There are many hard days ahead for me. I know not if I'll be healed or if I'll succumb to cancer. More than anything, I pray for faith so that I would keep my eyes on Jesus and walk through these raging waters without fear or despair. I pray for healing, yes, but I pray for faith even more urgently. Without faith there is no joy in healing. Without faith, any healing will only be seen ultimately as the inevitable being delayed. I pray, therefore, for faith!"

When they got into the boat, the wind ceased

Notice how the wind and the waves did *not* lessen while Peter was out on the water. Only after they got into the boat did the winds cease, not before.

I see this as a parallel to life and death. While we're alive here on earth, the winds and waves will rage against us. But after we die and come to be with the Lord, the winds will cease.

This is a key to our astonishing hope! Not only will the winds cease when we come to heaven, but we will also see God face to face. With 100% clarity we will perceive the glory of Christ Jesus as the Son of God and worship him face to face! Faith will no longer be necessary, let alone a fight. Our habitation will be with God, forever.

Let's not forget this suffering of ours is temporary. The winds *will* cease. We also must hold onto this astonishing hope that even if we die, we actually will *never* die. We will always be with the Lord forever in a land of incredible peace and calm.

"Raise a Hallelujah" by Bethel Music came on my playlist immediately after I first wrote the previous words. I took that as a "sign from the Lord" for me. I don't require signs from the Lord, but I cherish them nonetheless when they come!

Maybe it's more than a sign, however—maybe it's also a call to all of us to sing a song of praise to the Lord even in the middle of the greatest storm we've ever had to endure. Here's a sample of the lyrics for "Raise a Hallelujah." I hope the Lord uses it to encourage you in your storm as well. Praise his name, even amidst the waves!

I'm gonna sing in the middle of the storm
Louder and louder, you're gonna hear my praises roar
Up from the ashes hope will arise
Death is defeated, the King is alive

I raise a hallelujah
  with everything inside of me

I raise a hallelujah
  I will watch the darkness flee

I raise a hallelujah
  in the middle of the mystery

I raise a hallelujah
  fear, you lost your hold on me

Prayer to the Lord

Lord Jesus, help me to keep my eyes on you. The
waves of cancer crash against me, and I fear. My
prognosis isn't great, and I become sad. I cry out
to you, oh Lord, for help! Rescue me from fear
and sadness! Draw near to me, oh Lord!

Lord, thank you for drawing near to me. Thank you for comforting me. Thank you for your pro-vision of grace and faith, helping me to endure all things. I pray for a renewal of faith within me; help me to never doubt your goodness toward me.

In Jesus' name, Amen.

Question to Consider

What will you do to keep your eyes on Jesus as the ravaging winds and waves of this life crash against you? (See the Epilogue for some tips.)

Day 16

Strength for the Powerless

Isaiah 40:28-31

Do you not know?
Have you not heard?
The Lord is the everlasting God,
the Creator of the whole earth.
He never becomes faint or weary;
there is no limit to his understanding.
He gives strength to the faint
and strengthens the powerless.
Youths may become faint and weary,
and young men stumble and fall,
but those who trust in the Lord
will renew their strength;
they will soar on wings like eagles;
they will run and not become weary,
they will walk and not faint.

(The following journal entry was written on the 2nd day of my radiation treatment. I left it in its original form so it could be a testimony to the kind of work the Holy Spirit can do in our hearts during the toughest times. To God be the glory.)

Have you not heard? The Lord is the everlasting *God*!

I think it's worth pondering for a moment that God is... *God*! Sovereign. Majestic. Powerful. A just judge. A loving Father. Our Savior.

We don't worship a whimsical spirit or an idol made of wood and bronze. We worship the Living God! And he is good, so good to those who seek first his righteousness.

Not only that, we see that "he gives strength to the faint and strength to the powerless"! I've never in my life felt more faint of heart and powerless over my circumstances than I do now.

Today, as I write this, it is Day 2 of radiation treatment. Here at the beginning of treatment I can only hope in God, but that hope is not in vain. I hope in a good God, a powerful God, a God that loves me. A God that is both powerful to save, and has already saved me. But, he is also powerful to heal, and if I'm honest, he has already healed me in a number of ways.

Never in my life have I felt so close to God; my spirit has been renewed within me and is inclined toward God like never before. Is that not a great miracle of spiritual healing? I pray for bodily healing with all earnestness, but I pray knowing I have been, am being, and will be, healed ultimately on the Day of the Lord. What an astonishing hope we have in Christ Jesus!

And yet, before cancer I didn't have this inclination toward daily dependence on the Lord. I was arrogant in my youth. Like the "young men [who] stumble and fall," I stumbled in a spectacular way when I received my diagnosis. *I am too young, at age 40, to get cancer!* Or so I thought.

The irony was that health was my idol. I was an obsessive weight lifter, runner, and healthy eater. I think the lesson for me was that when we make a god out of something that is not the one true Living God, he will step in and renew a right spirit within us.

That's what God did in me—he renewed my soul to be inclined toward him. And despite being the sickest I've ever been, I feel the most alive that I've ever felt.

This is Isaiah's basic conclusion: the Lord renews the strength of those who trust in him. I wasn't trusting in him for my health, so he intervened. And now, like never before, I cast my fate on the Lord and I am strengthened at the perfect time, strengthened for the long and difficult road that is set before me.

Trust in the Lord and you will not grow weary. Cry out to the Lord day by day, moment by moment even, and he will strengthen you. Pray to the Lord ceaselessly and he will draw near to you. He will strengthen you. This is the essence of the astonishing hope we find in Isaiah 40.

The Lord will strengthen you.

The Lord will set your heart on the eagle's wings.
The Lord will make sure you do not grow weary.

Prayer to the Lord

Lord God, in your matchless sovereignty I hope and trust! Renew my strength, oh Lord, for the road I walk is difficult and my strength is insufficient. But the strength you supply, oh Lord, is enough to enable me to endure with patience, joy, and hope. Draw near to me in my weakness, oh God, for to whom else can I go for everlasting strength? Nobody compares to you, Lord. To you be the glory, forever.

In Jesus' name, Amen.

Question to Consider

Is God using a cancer diagnosis to renew a right spirit in you? How has your trust in the Lord grown or changed since first hearing of the diagnosis?

Day 17

God is Our Comfort

2 Corinthians 1:3-4

Blessed be the God and Father of our Lord Jesus Christ, the Father of mercies and the God of all comfort. He comforts us in all our afflictions, so that we may be able to comfort those who are in any kind of affliction, through the comfort we ourselves receive from God.

The ups and downs of cancer can feel like a rollercoaster. I remember one day early on when I had the opportunity to spend some sweet moments with my wife and children, and was also greatly encouraged by some time I spent with a brother who drove me to my treatment.

The next morning, however, I felt very sad. I was thankful for the memory of blessed moments like the ones I had the day before, to be sure. But when I thought about them, I also felt sad at the thought of possibly not having many moments like that in my future.

And yet, on that day, by God's providence, 2 Corinthians 1:3-4 was next on my list to journal through.

In our moments of despair we need to remember God draws near to us when we cry out to him. God is the Father of mercies and the God of all comfort, which means that all comfort comes from him and through him as an expression of his mercy and love toward us.

Let fear and despair be a wake-up call to pray. Don't sit in fear or despair, but rather war against it through prayer to the God of Comfort, and you will be comforted. And this comfort isn't only for our own benefit. Paul says in verse 4 that God comforts us so that we can comfort and help others in their affliction. We are not to be found hoarding the comfort God has given us.

In my own experience I have been comforted the most by talking with other believers who also have walked through cancer. My wife too has sought out other women whose husbands have had cancer and she was greatly encouraged. The church is the hands and feet of Christ and often the conduit of God's comfort for those who suffer.

At times God comforts us directly, like that morning when he answered my prayers for comfort in my sadness. But at other times his comfort comes through people. So we should pray that God will likewise use us to bring comfort to others. I've already seen how my sharing of the hope I have in Christ during cancer can be a powerful testimony of comfort to others who are suffering.

Let's not be greedy with the comfort we receive, but rather let it overflow to all those whom the Lord puts in our path. Let the people around you see the hope you have in Christ Jesus. Comfort them with verses, truths, prayers, and songs of praise. Encourage them to have their elders pray for them and anoint them with oil. Weep with them. Rejoice with them.

The essence of loving someone well is to walk with them in their suffering. Let love therefore go forth from you and may the God of Comfort use you mightily in the ministry of his mercy to others who suffer.

Prayer to the Lord

> *Father God, I cry out to you! I am fearful of dying, and I'm deeply saddened at the prospect of saying goodbye to these wonderful people you've put in my life. Comfort me, Father, and hear my cries for mercy! Draw near to me, oh Lord.*
>
> *God of Comfort, thank you for comforting me. Father of Mercy, thank you for showing me mercy. Thank you for the astonishing hope I have in Christ Jesus. I know that no matter what I will live forever with you, and with my family.*

Praise hallelujah! Grant me opportunities to share this comfort that I have received. May many be comforted with the comfort that I have received from you, Lord.

In Jesus, name, Amen.

Question to Consider

To whom are you a conduit of comfort that God is using to pour out an overflow of his comfort from you onto others?

Day 18

Childlike Faith

Matthew 18:3-5, 12-14

"Truly I tell you," he said, "unless you turn and become like little children, you will never enter the kingdom of heaven. Therefore, whoever humbles himself like this child—this one is the greatest in the kingdom of heaven. And whoever welcomes one child like this in my name welcomes me....

"See to it that you don't despise one of these little ones, because I tell you that in heaven their angels continually view the face of my Father in heaven. What do you think? If someone has a hundred sheep, and one of them goes astray, won't he leave the ninety-nine on the hillside and go and search for the stray? And if he finds it, truly I tell you, he rejoices over that sheep more than over the ninety-nine that did not go astray. In the same way, it is not the will of your Father in heaven that one of these little ones perish."

Jesus tells us that only those with a childlike faith will be saved. It's an incredible saying. A few verses later he also says that God desires all to be saved. Pride, it seems, is what stands in the way. Let's take a closer look at what we can learn from this passage.

The Lord desires our salvation

He uses the analogy here of a shepherd that leaves the 99

sheep to search after the one who left the flock. The one who left the flock is in great danger, even if that sheep is unaware of that fact.

For me personally, this analogy hits home. For many years prior to my cancer diagnosis, I was described by my friends as a "functional atheist." I was backslidden and self-reliant. Though I had some measure of faith in Jesus and God was definitely faithful toward me during these years, I was not relying on God or seeking him diligently. I was on a wayward path, and I didn't even know it.

I don't believe that the Lord caused my cancer, *per se*, but he has used it mightily to draw me back into the sheepfold and his presence. I went from having grave doubts about the Lord's existence to experiencing his tangible comforting presence, both bodily and spiritually. But I know my heart prior to cancer was too hardened to walk in the Holy Spirit. I behaved as if I didn't need God.

However, God didn't want me to be lost, so he saved me through the means he knew was best given my hardness of heart; he saved me through the fiery trial of cancer.

God loved me so much that he pulled out all the stops necessary to bring me back into the sheepfold. And now I know there is much rejoicing in heaven at my repentance. And there is much rejoicing on earth too, for now that I've tasted and seen God, I can never go back. I will forever be grateful for how God used cancer to awaken me from the danger I never knew I was in. Perhaps you too have a similar story.

He saves us by humbling us

What often gets in the way of our salvation? Is it not our pride? Intrinsically, you cannot be relying on God if you are relying on yourself. Self-reliance is the hallmark of pride and the biggest problem for those who have wandered from the flock and are lost as a result.

Pride can come in many forms. Pride can manifest by self-reliance in one's own provision for oneself, like your career, status, or wealth. This is what my pride often looks like. I don't need God because I can take care of myself.

Pride also often relies on one's own works. I don't need God, we may say, because I'm a good person; look at all these things I'm doing in Jesus' name to earn my salvation! Here we are relying on ourselves for our salvation versus relying on God's work through the death of Jesus to pay the price for our sins. Legalism and works-based righteousness of this sort is rampant in religion (and Christianity for that matter), and it doesn't save anybody.

Pride is at the root of what keeps people from salvation. Because they seemingly don't need God, they don't choose God. They are lost and they remain lost in their pride.

Cancer has shattered my pride. You lose all control over your life when you are diagnosed with cancer. For me this loss of control was a death sentence to my pride. I had nothing on which to stand within myself; I could only turn to Jesus. I went from self-sufficient to desperately dependent on God.

I think this kind of thing happens often when Jesus "leaves the flock" to pursue us when we have gone astray. In pride we think we can do it alone, but God shows us the truth of the matter when he intervenes to bring us back in.

He is conforming our faith to that of a child's_

Jesus tells us in these verses that our faith needs to be like that of a child's or we will *not* enter into the kingdom of heaven. These are startling words and we need to understand them.

The most defining characteristic of a child is their dependence on their parents for everything. It's no surprise that immediately after stating we need to be like children, Jesus says, "Therefore humble yourselves." Humility is a defining characteristic of a child and of the saved Christian.

Humility is also a defining characteristic of the cancer patient. Could it be that God is using cancer to conform our faith to be more like that of a child, fully dependent upon the Lord for everything?

My experience with cancer speaks this truth like a bullhorn. Nothing is so life-shattering, destabilizing, and gut-wrenching as getting a diagnosis of cancer. All my self-reliance dissolved in a moment. All my pride in my career, achievements, possessions, wealth, etc. evaporated overnight. They became meaningless, worthless. The only meaning left for me was the comfort, joy, protection, and provision I received from the Lord. Like a baby drinking milk, the presence of the Lord was all I wanted.

For the first time in my life I understood the "simple" faith of the child. Children believe in the love and goodness of their parents. They don't question it. They are also dependent on them for everything.

And that's it. That's the faith to which we are called.

Children reside in their parents' love and go to them for all their needs and wants. That's it. No long list of laws, no rules to follow to earn their love.

God likewise loves us unconditionally. The yoke and the burden the Lord puts on our shoulders to bear is "light" and easy to carry (Matthew 11:28-30).

The prideful cannot enter heaven, however, but only those who walk in childlike humility. The self-reliant cannot be saved, but only those who cling desperately to the Lord.

In this way I can be grateful for cancer, because through it I've returned to the sheepfold of Christ Jesus. My pride was shattered in such a way that was only possible through cancer because of my hardness of heart in my self-sufficiency.

Your story may be different, but I do think Jesus' analogy of childlike faith is applicable to everybody in some way or another. The bottom line is that we ought to reside in the love of God for us and depend on him for everything we need.

Prayer to the Lord

Father in heaven, thank you for loving me. Thank you for revealing yourself to me. Thank you for saving me. I trust in you for my salvation and for everything. I need you, Father—draw near to me, my Lord! Thank you for drawing near to me. I worship you.

In Jesus' name, Amen.

Question to Consider

Where is pride rooted in your life? How would God want you to dig it out and thereby become more childlike in your faith?

Day 19

Entrust Yourself to God

1 Peter 4:19

Let those who suffer according to God's will entrust themselves to a faithful Creator while doing what is good.

We are told there will be suffering in our lifetimes. A few verses earlier Peter makes this clear (verses 12-13):

> Dear friends, don't be surprised when the fiery ordeal comes among you to test you, as if something unusual were happening to you. Instead, rejoice as you share in the sufferings of Christ, so that you may also rejoice with great joy when his glory is revealed.

The context here is Christian persecution, but it applies to suffering of all kinds, such as cancer.

We shouldn't be surprised when affliction comes. We live in a fallen world ravaged by sin. But there's still great hope for us; Peter even goes so far as to suggest we can *rejoice* when we share in the sufferings of Christ. God came to earth bodily; he knows our pain. But one day his glory will be revealed fully to all people, which will be the cause of even more joy for those who trust in him. On that day our suffering will give way to a weight of glory that cannot be compared to this momentary affliction (2 Corinthians 4:17-18).

Therefore let us entrust ourselves to God. Why? Because God is the faithful Creator of the universe. He has a good plan for us. He'll carry us, just like he had a good plan for Job and carried Job through all Job's afflictions (Job 1:22).

Our trust in God also opens the door to our doing good despite being afflicted with cancer. It's really hard to love and serve others when we are wracked with fear and doubt. But when the peace of God overshadows our fear and doubt, we are enabled to overflow in good works. This is Peter's charge to us: trust God because he's a faithful creator and do not stop loving and serving others. We are waging a battle in our bodies, but it's a spiritual battle as well. Good works, as an overflow of our trust in God, should be just as much a part of our daily routines as our treatments for cancer.

God is faithful. He will carry you through this affliction. Trust him, and do not cease in your outpouring of love toward others. This is our calling to endurance during these difficult days. Cancer may plague your physical health, but don't let it ruin your spiritual health. Love others well with every day you are given.

Prayer to the Lord

> *Father God, you are the Lord over all things, the creator of the universe, and you are faithful. Help me, Father, to trust in you. Help me to patiently endure this trial, and to continue to abide in your presence through it all. I pray my love for others during this battle would not grow cold but would actually grow warmer as I share the hope I have in Christ Jesus. Use me, oh Lord, for your purposes.*
>
> *In Jesus' name, Amen.*

Question to Consider

> *Has it been difficult to trust in God during your battle with cancer? If trust has come easily, rejoice and thank God for the peace you have! If trust has been hard, cry out to the Lord that he would draw near to you and hold you by his righteous right hand (Isaiah 41:10, 13).*

Day 20

Be Strong and Courageous

Deuteronomy 31:6

Be strong and courageous. Do not fear or be in dread of them, for it is the Lord your God who goes with you. He will not leave you or forsake you.

There's a lot of truth and hope for us in this singular verse in Deuteronomy. In a nutshell, we ought to cast off fear. Why? Because God is with us. But there's so much more in the verse.

We are told to be strong. Strength in this context is strength of mind and spirit, which is good, because often physical strength cannot be relied upon. Our minds, however, aside from challenges with neurological disability or disease, can be a powerful weapon against the enemy.

Scientifically speaking, even the placebo effect has been shown to have a powerful effect on cancer symptoms such as fatigue and nausea. If we mentally give in to our symptoms, they will likely be heightened. If we focus on thoughts of optimism and hope, our symptoms will probably be lessened, even if still present. But for Christians this isn't just self-help mumbo-jumbo—our strength comes from the Lord and is powerful to give us hope far beyond any placebo effect.

We also must be courageous and not fear. As we saw in the Day 1 entry, fear is a powerful enemy. But here again we see a call to "not fear or be in dread of them." In the case of the Israelites, "them" refers to enemy armies, but we can apply it to our dread of cancer.

I'm reminded of the story of Gideon, who with 300 soldiers defeated over a hundred thousand. "Dread" would have been an assumed response against such odds. Obviously all 300 would die. Sometimes with cancer we too can just assume it's a death sentence and forget the power of God to heal, or allow the dread to stifle our joy in the promise of eternal life.

The reality is that death has been defeated. Jesus defeated it. You will *not* die from cancer. This is God's promise for us! Even the worst-case scenario, your body dying, doesn't change the fact that *you* will not die. *You* are more than a body, a shell; your consciousness, your spirit, your soul, will never die if you are in Christ Jesus.

None of this is to take away from the power of the name of Jesus to preserve our bodies for a while longer if that's his plan for us. But the bottom line is we need not fear. God is powerful to save us, and importantly, he will *never* leave us. God will *not* forsake you!

As a reminder, which we all need often in the fight against cancer, recall Isaiah 41:10-13. Jesus is reaching out to you with his righteous right hand, offering courage and strength in your battle:

> So do not fear, for I am with you; do not be dismayed, for I am your God. I will strengthen you and help you; I will uphold you with my righteous right hand.... For I am the LORD, your God, who takes hold of your right hand and says to you, "Do not fear; I will help you."

The call here is to cling to Jesus every moment of every day. When fear rises up, call out to God for courage! When symptoms feel overwhelming, call out to God for strength! Never stop calling on the name of Jesus as you fight for faith during this fiery trial!

Prayer to the Lord

> *Lord Jesus, draw near to me! I am afraid. Give me courage, Lord! Grab hold of me by your righteous right hand and sustain me. Strengthen my mind and soul to fight this fight for faith against this foe of cancer. You, oh Lord, are far*

mightier than cancer. You will never leave me or forsake me. Thank you for your presence, oh Lord, and for the gift of faith.

In Jesus' name, Amen.

Question to Consider

Are there any negative feelings in your mind or body that you are not warring against? As a personal example, I often fall into sullenness without even knowing it, sometimes realizing it not until hours or days later, when I then acknowledge my sadness and pray for joy. Sorrow is normal, to be expected, but I desire to be sorrowful yet always rejoicing. I certainly do not want to remain unaware of my sorrow, lest I find myself not fighting the fight of faith.

Day 21

God is With Us in Our Fiery Trial

Daniel 3:23-25

And these three men, Shadrach, Meshach, and Abednego fell, bound, into the furnace of blazing fire. Then King Nebuchadnezzar jumped up in alarm. He said to his advisers, "Didn't we throw three men, bound, into the fire?" "Yes, of course, Your Majesty," they replied to the king. He exclaimed, "Look! I see four men, not tied, walking around in the fire unharmed; and the fourth looks like a son of the gods."

I love the book of Daniel. It shows us that God isn't surprised by anything. His plans will stand; his prophecies will be fulfilled. God will redeem this fallen world.

Daniel served several kings during the Babylonian exile, during which the nation of Israel was conquered and carried off to Babylon as slaves. Daniel tells the story of three Jewish men who refused to worship King Nebuchadnezzar, and for this Nebuchadnezzar threw them into a furnace to be burned to death.

For these three men, this was quite literally a fiery trial! But what was more important to these men, their love for their lives or their love for God? They could have easily saved their lives by bowing down. But they didn't; they loved God more than life itself.

In my opinion this is the most amazing aspect of the story. Obviously the miracle of not getting burned is amazing in itself, but these men didn't know they would be saved. We see in verses 17-18 that they knew God *could* save them if he wanted to, but even if he didn't, they still would not bow down. They were unsure if they would live or die, and yet they still chose not to worship anything other than God. Here's what they said to the King:

> He can rescue us from the furnace of blazing fire, and he can rescue us from the power of you, the king. But even if he does not rescue us, we want you as king to know that we will not serve your gods or worship the gold statue you set up.

Their courage never faltered, even when staring death in the face. What an example for those of us whose future is filled with uncertainty.

What's also amazing is the fact that God was with them in the midst of the fire. The pre-incarnate Jesus stood with them in the fire. They were not alone in their fiery trial. Neither are you or I alone in our fiery trial of cancer.

If God is powerful enough to save these men from a furnace, with not a single hair on their bodies singed, then he is powerful enough to save us even from cancer. Like Shadrach, Meshach, and Abendigo, we may not know if he'll heal our bodies or not, but we will *not* bow down to other gods, gods of fear, sullenness, or hopelessness, or any other god of this world that causes us to doubt or turn away from the hope we have in Christ Jesus.

Satan is trying to draw us toward hopelessness, because hopelessness whittles away at the power of God in our lives. But we need not go there. We have hope in God during this fiery trial. In fact, God has *already* saved us if we are in Christ. And God will save us again on the last day. When Jesus comes again to earth, our spirits in heaven will be moved into our resurrected physical bodies and we will live on this earth again, bodily, as we do now but perfected, forever!

This is our astonishing hope, friends. It was clearly the hope of Shadrach, Meshach and Abendigo. They knew of their salvation. They did not fear the fire. Nor should we fear it!

Jesus stands at your side in this moment, and always. Seek and feel the presence of your great God. He is with you. He is next to you. He is dwelling within you. He will never leave you.

Prayer to the Lord

Lord Jesus, thank you for drawing near to me. Thank you for standing with me during this fiery trial of cancer. Thank you for giving me great hope in salvation and the resurrection of my body! Strengthen this hope, oh Lord. Bless me with more of your spirit within me so that this hope would grow ever brighter every day. May others see the hope that I have in you and likewise come to believe in your great name and your great power to save.

In Jesus' name, Amen.

Question to Consider

If you were offered a cure for your cancer, but you had to deny Jesus, would you take it? Or to put it another way, if your cancer became terminal, would you doubt the love of God for you?

Day 22

Count Trials as Joy

James 1:2-12

Consider it a great joy, my brothers and sisters, whenever you experience various trials, because you know that the testing of your faith produces endurance. And let endurance have its full effect, so that you may be mature and complete, lacking nothing.

Now if any of you lacks wisdom, he should ask God—who gives to all generously and ungrudgingly—and it will be given to him. But let him ask in faith without doubting. For the doubter is like the surging sea, driven and tossed by the wind. That person should not expect to receive anything from the Lord, being double-minded and unstable in all his ways.

Let the brother of humble circumstances boast in his exaltation, but let the rich boast in his humiliation because he will pass away like a flower of the field. For the sun rises and, together with the scorching wind, dries up the grass; its flower falls off, and its beautiful appearance perishes. In the same way, the rich person will wither away while pursuing his activities.

Blessed is the one who endures trials, because when he has stood the test he will receive the crown of life that God has promised to those who love him.

The first two verses of that passage are often quoted to sufferers as if we ought to automatically know what benefit endurance has for the sufferer. (Other translations use the words "perseverance," "steadfastness," and "patience.") But why should our growth in endurance be a joyful occasion?

The answer may be different for everybody. I'm going to share my experience as an example, but I realize that everybody experiences suffering differently and I don't want to project my experience onto others as some sort of standard. It is not.

Prior to cancer, my faith was essentially untested. I lived a privileged life without any major challenges. I've always had faith to some degree or another, but have never really needed to exercise it until now.

When the trial comes, will our faith be found to be deeply-rooted and life-giving or shallow-rooted and unreliable? I honestly never really knew what it meant to rely on God before cancer, and only now can I see how deep God was rooting me even without me knowing it.

The trial of cancer has yielded for me endurance, steadfastness, and patience like never before. It is a joy to know the Lord's presence. It's a joy to be carried by the Lord's righteous right hand. Once you've met the living God, there's no turning back.

I was recently asking a friend why this trial yielded me joy, while for others it can often be devastating, causing people to curse God and fall away from him. I honestly don't know the answer to that question, but what I do know is that asking it causes me to be even more thankful for the hope my trial has birthed within me.

It didn't have to be this way. I didn't choose joy in cancer. What happened, for me at least, is that God just showed up as if out of nowhere and the peace of God that surpasses understanding (Philippians 4:7) was manifest for me, resulting in a depth of joy I had never known before.

Verses 4-12 of James 1 are often left out of the picture when verses 2-3 are quoted. However, they add important clarity when considering the importance of endurance and why it yields joy.

We see how endurance is connected to wisdom. We know from elsewhere in the Bible that the fear of the Lord is the beginning of wisdom (Proverbs 9:10). Again, for me personally, I saw the hand of the Lord in my diagnosis, in that God turned something evil for my good to bring me back to him after my waywardness and growing doubts.

I was reminded of the power of God, the sovereignty of God, and the worthiness of God for my life to be employed toward fruitful work for his glory. Today, I tremble at the thought of wasting whatever precious time I have left. I think this trembling, this fear, is the beginning of wisdom in me.

We also see the doubter being tossed about by the wind in verse 6. Trials have a way of being used by God to plant us on solid rock (and give us the steadfastness to hold on to it). Cancer can feel like a hurricane, but when we rely on God and seek first his righteousness, there's a peace of God that can increasingly characterize us. Unlike the doubter, we who are held by the righteous right hand of God are steadfast amidst the torrents of wind and rain. Our trial, Lord willing, will cause joy to well up inside us because of the sturdy, solid rock of hope that we have in Christ Jesus.

Finally, the effect of endurance is that we'll lack nothing. Our riches will fail us (verse 11). However, if we endure until the end, we will be given everything.

"Blessed is the one who endures trials, because when he has stood the test he will receive the crown of life that God has promised to those who love him" (v. 12). A crown symbolizes possession. We will possess life forevermore.

Therefore, consider it joy when you face trials of various kinds.

Prayer to the Lord

Heavenly Father, grab hold of me by your righteous right hand. Draw near to me, oh Lord, and plant me on the solid rock of your love and your promises. Turn this evil I'm facing for my good by giving me steadfastness and patience to endure with wisdom until the day of my glorification and fullness of joy in your presence. Moreover, fill me anew with your Holy

*Spirit and your peace so that joy would super-
naturally characterize my life, for I know such
joy amidst difficult circumstances is a gift from
God alone, and so I ask for my joy to be made full
while I patiently wait for the Lord.*

In Jesus' name, Amen.

Question to Consider

*Is untested faith real? How can one know if their
faith is real if it has never been tested? How
blessed are we whose faith has been proven reliable!*

Day 23

Finding Rest in Simple Faith

Matthew 11:28-30

*Come to me, all of you who are weary and bur-
dened, and I will give you rest. Take up my yoke
and learn from me, because I am lowly and
humble in heart, and you will find rest for your
souls. For my yoke is easy and my burden is light.*

In those verses the Lord Jesus uses the analogy of oxen that
are "yoked" with a heavy burden (the yoke is what connects the
oxen to the wagon or plow). He calls us to cast off our burdens
and find rest in him.

Cancer is a heavy burden. I have grown weary while carry-
ing it. The burden was heaviest when I had weeks and months
ahead of me that would involve a lot of fatigue, nausea, difficulty swallowing, vomiting and reflux, followed by a surgery (if
all went well). After all that I would be left with a feeding tube
and a liquid diet for months. And regardless of that excruci-
ating treatment, just knowing I had cancer in my body was
itself a wearying burden.

Jesus implies that we cannot carry both our burdens and
the Lord's yoke at the same time. An ox is connected to one
load, not two. I cannot carry a yoke of worry about cancer, for
example, and carry the yoke of the Lord's rest at the same
time.

He also implies that the way we can get rid of our unnecessary and harmful burdens is to trade them for his yoke and
teaching, which means to commit ourselves to obeying him
according to what he says in the Word. My physical symptoms
may not necessarily improve when I take off my yoke and put
on the Lord's, but my attitude always will! And my peace. And

joy. And so on.

When I carry the Lord's yoke, my soul finds the rest Jesus promises me. However, if I later take up the yoke of my troubles again, I inevitably return to the sullenness and despair caused by my circumstances. The ebb and flow between these two yokes is the result of a war waged in my soul between despair and joy, peace and worry.

This battle extends to my motivations as well.

At the height of my cancer struggle I spent almost an entire weekend researching seminaries I could attend. I was obsessing about setting out on a course of deep study and maybe becoming a pastor or a full-time Christian author.

Some of this arose from my new-found zeal for God, my love for him, and my desire to serve him in all the remaining days of my life. However, later that weekend the Spirit rebuked me with Psalm 46:10: "Be still and know that I am God." The idea of seminary, while a noble pursuit for many people, was my idea, not God's. There was also a root inside me of desiring my own glory and renown. I also tend to want to load myself up with as heavy of a burden as possible and grow discontent if I'm not weary enough. Endless striving for accomplishment and achievement has been a common feature of my life.

The Spirit was telling me, however, that I'm in a season where burdensome toil isn't what God wants from me, but rather he was simply calling me to be still and know that he is God. The Lord's yoke is light, after all, and he is offering us rest.

When I shared this with a dear friend of mine, he gave me the analogy of the motorcycle with a sidecar. He said that Jesus is driving the motorcycle and I'm in the sidecar along for the ride. If the Lord wants me to do X, Y, or Z, he will take me there.

We are never entirely passive in our spiritual lives, but that analogy hits an important note about the simple nature of faith. We are not the ones in charge of where we're going, nor do we have the ability to get there by ourselves. And our part in the journey is not complicated. Jesus says the essence of his law is to love God and love people and that's it. The whole of the law—how we should live in response to his grace—is wrapped up in those two simple commands (Mark 12:30-31). And yet we too often focus on esoteric doctrines, extra-biblical rules, and other distractions from the essence of what God is calling us to do.

Jesus is the author and finisher of our faith (Hebrews 12:2). We're called to love God and love people like he did. That's it... fairly simple and definitely not burdensome, especially since he gives us his Spirit as our Helper.

Whatever God has for your future, you'll get to it when he wants you to get to it (God's timing is another source of rest for us). When God wants you to preach, teach, or do X, Y or Z, he will lead you there. I believe this. It's not your job to get yourself from A to Z. God will get you there, whatever "there" is for you.

Therefore (no pun intended), take up the yoke of Jesus and find rest. Pursue loving the Lord and others with your whole heart, mind, and strength, and then hop in the sidecar of God's plan for your life and see what roads the Lord may take you down. You'll find that he'll take you to some places you yourself could never have anticipated.

Prayer to the Lord

Lord Jesus, thank you for the rest I have in you. Thank you for calling me to rest in your presence and not to burdensome toil. Thank you that I can cast off the burden of cancer onto you, and that you give me peace and even joy amidst the sorrows of this great evil in my life. Use my life, oh Lord, for your glory and my joy. I'm hopping in your proverbial sidecar; take me where you want me to go.

In Jesus' name, Amen.

Question to Consider

What is a yoke (burden or effort) in your life that you have not yet cast off and given to the Lord to do with as he pleases?

Day 24

One Day at a Time

Matthew 6:25-34

Therefore I tell you: Don't worry about your life, what you will eat or what you will drink; or about your body, what you will wear. Isn't life more than food and the body more than clothing? Consider the birds of the sky: They don't sow or reap or gather into barns, yet your heavenly Father feeds them. Aren't you worth more than they? Can any of you add one moment to his life span by worrying? And why do you worry about clothes? Observe how the wildflowers of the field grow: They don't labor or spin thread. Yet I tell you that not even Solomon in all his splendor was adorned like one of these. If that's how God clothes the grass of the field, which is here today and thrown into the furnace tomorrow, won't he do much more for you—you of little faith? So don't worry, saying, "What will we eat?" or "What will we drink?" or "What will we wear?" For the Gentiles eagerly seek all these things, and your heavenly Father knows that you need them. But seek first the kingdom of God and his righteousness, and all these things will be provided for you. Therefore don't worry about tomorrow, because tomorrow will worry about itself. Each day has enough trouble of its own.

Jesus asks us to do three things in these verses: 1) seek first the kingdom of God, 2) live in the moment, and 3) not worry. One leads to the next, and all three are dependent upon each other if we're to do them faithfully.

Worry is one of the biggest temptations during cancer. It's so easy to fear the worst.

I remember a day one week before a PET scan that would determine whether I could have surgery the following day. If metastasis was found on the scan, that would mean my cancer was inoperable and my surgery would be canceled. It was easy to worry about the results of the scan, and I knew from experience that such anxiety, left unchecked, could easily debilitate me and steal away the joy of precious moments that God had for me in the coming days. Satan wants to use worry to rob us of the presence of God himself.

But praise God for his Son Jesus and his loving words for us! He has provided a path away from worry. He doesn't just say, "Don't worry about tomorrow," but shows us *how* we can overcome anxiety.

Freedom from worry starts with knowing we're not citizens of this world, but citizens of the Kingdom of God. God's kingdom is not of this world, but is still present in this world. Wherever the church is gathered and wherever the Holy Spirit moves, the kingdom of God is present.

We're told to seek first this kingdom—not our healing, pleasures, riches, or comforts. Seeking first the kingdom of God means to seek to dwell with our Lord in spirit, truth, and the community of believers. It means to commune with God and our brothers and sisters in Christ, and to build up his church, which is the earthly manifestation of the kingdom in this present age. This is our highest calling in life, and whether God gives us just one more day or 10,000 more days, the calling remains the same.

We are also told to live in the moment. Jesus says that each day has enough trouble of its own. Personally, when it comes to cancer, it's far easier for me to live in the future, such as worrying about an upcoming scan, than to live in the moment. It's also far easier to live in the past, such as analyzing what I did wrong with my diet or environment to get cancer in the first place. But either living in the past or future is folly and a waste of our precious lives.

Jesus says that God knows what we need; he knows the

future. Also, God doesn't make mistakes; he is turning our cancer for our good, preparing us for good works that give us joy and give him glory.

The past and the future are in God's hands and it doesn't do us any good to worry about them. I know that God has the entire universe in the palm of his hands; so I could trust that he had my upcoming PET scan in his hands too. Compared with eternal joy in his presence, the results of a scan seem trivial. Likewise, I need not worry about my past. God has led me to this place for my good and his glory.

Worrying isn't going to add a single day to our lives, Jesus says. God knows our days and knows how he plans to use us. He has good plans for you, so don't worry about anything. Live each and every day for itself. Live in the moment. Be a blessing to those around you. Take captive every minute of every day to share the hope you have in Christ Jesus with those around you. In so doing you're laying up for yourself treasure in heaven which neither moth nor rust (nor cancer) can ever destroy.

In fact, worrying about the future (or regretting the past) steals not just your present joy, but also your eternal joy, when that effort could instead be used to build up the church, the kingdom of God. Such work is rewarded. Don't miss an opportunity for an extra measure of eternal joy because of worrying.

Finally, consider Lamentations 3:22-23 as yet another call to take it one day at a time: "The steadfast love of the Lord never ceases; his mercies never come to an end; they are new every morning; great is your faithfulness."

Amen!

Prayer to the Lord

> *Father God, help me not to worry about the future or regret the past. Thank you for the blood of Christ Jesus, who paid for my regrets and purchased my future with him forevermore. Help me to take it one day at a time, each and every day seeking your presence, your Holy Spirit, and seeking to be a blessing to those you've put in my*

life. Help me, by your Spirit, not to waste any of the precious days you give me.

In Jesus' name, Amen.

Question to Consider

In what way is the Lord calling you to build his kingdom here on earth and be a blessing to others, which will also deliver you from fear and worry?

Day 25

You Are Not Alone

Matthew 28:20

And remember, I am with you always, to the end of the age.

(Below is a journal entry, in its original form, that I wrote as I waited the necessary six weeks for surgery after my treatment ended. It was a lonely time, and perhaps if you feel lonely, it will be an encouragement to you.)

Today, and for the last week or so, I have felt lonely. The busyness of life tends to pull everyone around me back into normalcy, but not me. I still think about my cancer all the time.

I'm not saying I want a big pity party day after day after day. I don't! Especially from my kids; I don't want them worried about me and I want them to live and enjoy life. Frankly, I want this for myself too. However, I'm finding that cancer can be quite isolating.

By God's providence, this verse came to me at a perfect time. It is a beautiful reminder that even in my isolation I am *not* alone. Jesus is with me, always, even until the very end.

"Uncle" Gary Lubben reminded me this morning, as I also happened upon this verse, that God will never give me something that is too hard to endure (1 Corinthians 10:13). This also reminded me of Philippians 4:13: "I can do all things through Christ who strengthens me."

Jesus is with me even if it feels like everybody around me has moved on. I am given the Spirit of Christ Jesus, not a spirit of fear. Likewise, God has not given me a spirit of loneliness, but one of power (1 Timothy 1:7).

I am not alone. I can endure all things. I have been given a spirit of power.

No pity party needed here!

It is well with my soul.

Prayer to the Lord

Jesus, thank you for your promise to be with me always. All those around me may fail me, but you, oh Lord, will never leave me. Draw near to me, Jesus.

In Jesus' name, Amen.

Question to Consider

Suffering can be isolating, as it makes those who are not suffering uncomfortable (most people work very hard not to think about death, for example). Do you know someone who is suffering that you can encourage and lift up?

Day 26

I Am the Resurrection and the Life

John 11:25-27

Jesus said to her, "I am the resurrection and the life. The one who believes in me, even if he dies, will live. Everyone who lives and believes in me will never die. Do you believe this?"

"Yes, Lord," she told him, "I believe you are the Messiah, the Son of God, who comes into the world."

At times it is helpful to contemplate death. If I had not been forced to contemplate my death, I would never have come to know the richness of hope found in Christ Jesus.

I was living in oblivion, knowing I'd die someday but never allowing myself to think about it. I had just assumed my death would be 40, 50, or even 60 years away. But that foolish assumption came crashing down one day.

Replacing it, however, by God's grace, was a supernatural hope. I discovered a solid foundation for my future expectations, and I'm better for it. Would I rather live another 50 years in oblivion, or would I rather live one more year in the certainty that I'll actually live forever?

In his words to Mary, Jesus makes the answer clear. Jesus conquered death. Death is defeated. 1 Corinthians 15:54 says, "Death has been swallowed up in victory." This victory is yours, too.

Jesus says even if you die, you will not actually die—you will live! Those in Christ *will never die*. Do you believe this? If you do, you are walking in Jesus' victory over death.

Romans 12:12 says we ought to rejoice in our hope, being patient in suffering and ceaseless in prayer. I think this is our calling as cancer sufferers. The hope of eternal life is an astonishing hope. Contemplating death in a cancer devotional seems a bit morbid, but the fact is everybody will die eventually. Except those of us who are in Christ Jesus! Isn't that incredible? You will never die, even if you die.

Contemplate that and *rejoice!* Give praise to God!

Because of this hope you can be patient in your suffering, and by the power of prayer you can patiently endure anything. Remember, these light and momentary affiliations are not worth comparing to the eternal weight of glory being prepared for you in heaven (2 Corinthians 4:17-18).

You are being prepared for the revealing of the full glory of Jesus Christ. This glory, this eternal life, is far beyond all comparison to the challenges you face in this present age.

This is a hard fact to grasp when cancer seems like a mountain of pain and fear. So I suggest that you constantly give thought to this: You will never die, if you are in Christ. And your future is so amazing that even the worst day of your life thus far will seem as a mere drop in the Pacific Ocean of glory and happiness that awaits you.

Do you believe this? If you struggle to believe, don't forget Paul's admonition toward "ceaseless prayer." Your faith will ebb and flow, but prayer will anchor you to the astonishing hope you have in Christ Jesus.

Prayer to the Lord

> *Father God, thank you for the hope that I have in Christ Jesus! Thank you for defeating death itself! Dying just means my glorification and the renewal of my body; praise hallelujah! Help me, father, to be patient in my suffering. Help me, Holy Spirit, to be ceaseless in prayer.*

> *In Jesus' name, Amen.*

Question to Consider

> *Has the contemplation of your death been*

mostly characterized by fear or by hope? If fear, pray to God that his promises for you would become deeply rooted in your spirit. If hope, praise God for his grace toward you.

Day 27

All Things for Good

Romans 8:28

We know that all things work together for the good of those who love God, who are called according to his purpose.

This verse can seem like a cliche when quoted to sufferers to encourage them. In the early weeks after my diagnosis, I was quoted this verse many times and, to be honest, I didn't find it that encouraging. Can cancer be for my good? I didn't feel very comforted, but as any good Minnesotan would do, I nodded and smiled and thanked them for their encouragement.

I waited to address this verse until near the end of the first 30 days because it took a while before I saw the truth in it. I never doubted it was true, *per se*, but I didn't initially believe that it was true for myself and my diagnosis. What I needed to see the truth of this verse in my circumstances was *time*. People quoting this verse to me fell flat early on because I was not yet able to look back and see what God was doing in my life. In those days I only saw the evil of cancer, not how God was turning it for my good.

Cancer has been the first major struggle of my life. I've had challenges, but nothing compares to this. And nothing compares to how I've since learned to rely on God. It took cancer for me to learn what it means to rely on God, to be totally dependent upon him for hope. All self-reliance was shattered when I was diagnosed, and God filled the void left with his presence. Hardness was shattered and faith was restored. Hope was established and rooted deeper than ever. I have never in my entire life been so certain of my salvation in Christ Jesus as I am now.

So here I sit with hindsight helping me see that indeed "all things work together for my good." I didn't see it in the first weeks of my diagnosis, but just two months later it was as obvious to me as the morning sunrise.

When sin entered the world, so did suffering. But that doesn't mean God is not able to turn suffering for our good, even if Satan means it for evil.

N.T. Wright, in his book *Into the Heart of Romans* (2023), suggests the translation "for our good" should really be "*with* our good," when you look closely at the original Greek. He says this removes unnecessary determinism from the text and helps us see how God, through his Spirit, works in and through us, and we likewise work in and through the power of the Spirit, to bring about "good" in this fallen world and to express our vocation as restorers of God's goodness and original purposes for his creation.

The takeaway for me here, personally speaking, is that both "for our good" and "with our good" could be true. I'm not an expert on Greek exegesis but I do know God *is* doing a thousand things in my life. However, to Wright's point, I also shouldn't sit idly by, passive, just waiting for this "good" to be revealed to me. I should be about my godly vocation of crying out to God in my suffering and also testifying of the astonishing hope that I have in Christ Jesus, and thereby, little by little, contributing to the restoration of the Kingdom of God here on earth.

My hope and prayer for you is that you will see the "good" in cancer soon, if you haven't already, and that you would be patient in waiting for it. God *is* doing a thousand things through your or your loved one's diagnosis that you cannot see, but the "big picture" will become more and more visible as time goes by.

Prayer to the Lord

Lord, I know that you are God. You hold the world in your hands. You, oh Lord, are working a thousand things in my life that I cannot even see, for you are sovereign over all. I can't fathom how cancer may be turned for my good, but I trust that you are able to do it. Use me, oh Lord, during this trial to be about the work of Christ in this world. May my life not be characterized by cancer, but rather by the work you've called me to. By your Holy Spirit, may I be a blessing to those around me as I share the good news of Christ.

In Jesus' name, Amen.

Question to Consider

In what ways could God be turning a cancer diagnosis around for your good? If you cannot see it yet, read the story of Joseph, who was sold into slavery by his brothers and yet God was able to turn that evil circumstance into the salvation of many from the famine that was to later strike the land (Genesis 37-50). Consider how Joseph was not an idle, passive actor in God's good plans for the people of Israel during the famine. Joseph was active, working with God throughout those years. How can God bring about good in your life and the lives around you?

Day 28

The Race Set Before Us

Hebrews 12:1-3

*Therefore, since we also have such a large cloud
of witnesses surrounding us, let us lay aside
every hindrance and the sin that so easily
ensnares us. Let us run with endurance the race
that lies before us, keeping our eyes on Jesus,
the pioneer and perfecter of our faith. For the joy
that lay before him, he endured the cross,
despising the shame, and sat down at the right
hand of the throne of God. For consider him who
endured such hostility from sinners against
himself, so that you won't grow weary and give
up.*

One morning during my treatment I did something I knew was
risky...I googled my cancer. Everybody on YouTube loves to
start a cancer conversation with survival rates, and I wish that
wasn't the case.

Who do they think benefits from discussions about survival rates? Are they trying to scare folks without cancer into not
getting something they have no control over getting? Or are
they trying to make those with the disease lose hope? I don't
see any benefit of discussing survival rates unless the explicit
topic is the survival rates themselves, which was obviously not
the content I was looking for. Even when the odds are very fav-
orable, the person often trusts in the odds themselves, which
is a shaky foundation to stand on at best. I don't know about
you, but I do not feel hopeful about putting my trust in a roll of
the dice.

In times like that Google session, fear would rise up in me

and I needed the promises of God to anchor me back into the astonishing hope that I have in Christ Jesus. In those moments, my eyes were taken off Jesus and instead I'm looking at my circumstances. Like Peter, I'm looking at the crashing waves instead of Christ and I start to sink and drown.

So that day I resolved to put aside every hindrance that so easily ensnares me. For me, trusting in the odds (or more accurately, despairing in the odds) is one of those hindrances. Is my hope rooted in the odds, or rooted in the goodness of God? Do I believe in the power of the name of Jesus to heal me or not? And even in the worst-case scenario, which is honestly nothing less than my joy made full, do I believe in the resurrection and perfection of my body (Philippians 3:20-4:1)? Oh how I need the promises of God to wash over me daily! Draw near to me, oh Lord!

Therefore, let us run with endurance the race that is set before us, keeping our eyes on Jesus, the author and perfecter of our faith!

I just feel like I need to say that again...

Therefore, let us run with endurance the race that is set before us, keeping our eyes on Jesus, the author and perfecter of our faith!

When Peter kept his eyes on Jesus he could walk on water, but when he took his eyes off Jesus he sank. This rings so true for me. Survival isn't being cured cancer; survival is keeping my eyes on Jesus!

Above all, consider Jesus. He too endured extreme hardship. In his case he endured persecution from sinners to the point of death. In our case, we must endure cancer. But Jesus knew the bigger purposes of God. He ran with endurance the race set before him because he knew God's plans for him must be fulfilled, which was nothing less than the salvation of the world.

We too should rest in knowing that God has good plans for us. He has set a race before us to run, and he will supply the strength we need to finish the race. If we look to Jesus each and every day, we will be strengthened to run our race with endurance and great hope, knowing our enduring is not in vain. In we are laying up for ourselves a reward in heaven, especially if our endurance overflows in love onto those around us.

There is still work yet for us to do. Run the race! Do not grow weary! Do not give up!

Look to Jesus!

Prayer to the Lord

Lord Jesus, keep my eyes on you so that I won't sink into despair. Keep reminding me daily of your promises to me, oh Lord. Draw near to me and comfort me, oh my mighty God! Help me to run this race and supply me with strength to endure to the end.

In Jesus' name, Amen.

Question to Consider

What is a hindrance in your life that you may need to set aside? Consider possessions, practices, fears, or even toxic people, and what practical changes you need to make.

Day 29

Prayer for Healing, Praise for Hope

Romans 12:12

Rejoice in hope; be patient in affliction; be persistent in prayer.

In this verse Paul tells us that we ought to rejoice in the hope we have in Christ Jesus. Rejoice!

To rejoice means to take joy in something and to give praise for that something. Hope is that something, according to Paul. For cancer sufferers this is a hope for healing, to be sure, but even more the hope we have for new bodies and eternal life.

Moreover, if we rejoice in hope and are persistent in prayer, we can have the strength to be patient in our affliction. Everybody with cancer knows how difficult patience can be. The waiting is the worst part. But hope and prayer produces patience. The opposite, which is fear and self-reliance, makes the waiting unbearable. But when we take strength in the hope we have in the promises of God and keep our eyes ceaselessly fixed on Jesus, we can endure with patience.

I'm also reminded by this verse that our rejoicing in hope is not only for our benefit, but for the encouragement of others. I found myself reminding my brothers and sisters in Christ, when they come over to my house for prayer, that in addition to praying for my healing we need to be praising God for my hope.

Hope in tribulation is a miracle, a gift from God. If you feel the hope rise up and the peace of God settling on your heart, make much of God for giving you that great gift. And if you do not feel the welling up of hope and peace in God, make *that* your main prayer request. Our bodies will fail all of us eventually, but our hope in God will never fail us.

Pray for faith. Fight for faith. Pray for healing to be sure, but pray even more, urgently and ceaselessly, for faith.

Prayer to the Lord

Lord Jesus, it's in the power of your name, oh Lord, that I pray for the healing of my body and the conquering of this cancer within me. Hear my cries for mercy, oh Lord. And yet, oh God, I also rejoice for the hope set before me in Christ Jesus. No matter what happens to me here on earth, I will be healed. My body will be glorified and lifted up. I will live forever. I pray for many more years on earth to sing your praises and to share with others the hope I have in Christ, but I also give praise to your name for this great hope I have in Jesus. I pray for a miracle in my body, and I give praise for the miracle in my heart. I pray you will continue to do this miracle in my heart. Let my faith not waver! Be faithful to me, oh Lord, because the enemy prowls around looking for opportunities to tempt me to fear. In Jesus' name I stand firm in the promises of God. May others see me stand and likewise be encouraged and give praise to your Holy Name.

In Jesus' name, Amen.

Question to Consider

Consider how rejoicing in hope, being patient in affliction, and being persistent in prayer may be mutually dependent upon one another. By the power of God's grace, strive to excel at all three.

Day 30

The Good Fight

1 Timothy 6:12

Fight the good fight of the faith. Take hold of eternal life to which you were called and about which you have made a good confession in the presence of many witnesses.

We are fighting for faith even more than we are fighting cancer. This has been the central theme through these first 30 days of meditations about God's promises.

It's a battle. It's not easy. Faith and fear ebb and flow. Some days we ride high on the promises of God and the hope we have in Christ Jesus. Some days, through many tears, we fear for our lives, sometimes even believing in the lies of the enemy.

It's a battle for faith. We must fight with all our might.

Paul also uses battle language in Ephesians 6:10-16, where he calls us to "take up the full armor of God." These verses tell us how to fight for faith even in the midst of dark and troubling waters:

> Finally, be strengthened by the Lord and by his vast strength. Put on the full armor of God so that you can stand against the schemes of the devil. For our struggle is not against flesh and blood, but against the rulers, against the authorities, against the cosmic powers of this darkness, against evil, spiritual forces in the heavens. For this reason take up the full armor of God, so that you may be able to resist in the evil day, and having prepared everything, to take your stand. Stand, therefore, with truth like a belt around your waist, righteousness

like armor on your chest, and your feet sandaled with readiness for the gospel of peace. In every situation take up the shield of faith with which you can extinguish all the flaming arrows of the evil one.

Here are some spiritual battle strategies from that passage and the one above it:

Stand in the truth

The promises of God are our sure foundation in the midst of cancer. If we believe in Jesus, we will be saved and raised from the dead (John 3:16, Romans 10:9). We have not been given a spirit of fear, but of power (2 Timothy 1:7). Cancer is being turned for our good and the good of many others too (Genesis 50:20, Philippians 1:6). This light and momentary affliction is making way for an eternal weight of glory beyond all comparison (2 Corinthians 4:17). God will not leave us nor forsake us (Deuteronomy 31:6). These and many other promises of God are what we need to stand in, and Jesus is the culmination of all of them. He is our solid rock and we eagerly await his appearing.

Clothe yourself in righteousness

We cannot serve two masters (Matthew 6:24). We cannot live for the desires of our flesh and still fight effectively for faith. Therefore, we are told to clothe ourselves in righteousness, so that no foothold of sin will take hold in our hearts and hinder our faith when we need it most. In Romans 13:14 Paul shows us what this looks like: "Put on the Lord Jesus Christ, and make no provision for the flesh to gratify its desires." We are to "put on" Jesus. Just as we carry the clothes on our backs all day long and even while we sleep, we are to put on Jesus, so that he goes with us wherever we go.

When we live in the presence of Christ, constantly thinking about him and serving him, Satan and the flesh will have no opportunity to tempt us. All our time and energy will be directed toward being like Christ.

Be ready with the gospel of peace

To keep "your "feet sandaled with readiness" means that you should be prepared to share your hope in Christ Jesus whenever a door to do so may be opened to you. The world needs this hope, and God allowed our suffering knowing it would yield the fruit of faith in ourselves but also in others we minister to. So always be ready. God may open the door of faith to even the most atheistic of those near you. Pain of loss can often break through the hardest of hearts.

Let faith be your shield

As I said, it's a fight for faith more than a fight against cancer. Of course it's both, but we fight cancer by fighting for faith. Faith is our shield during the shock of receiving the diagnosis. Faith is our shield as we're logging into our health records to see the pathology results. Faith is our shield amidst the fear as we're being wheeled into the operating room for a complicated surgery. Faith is our shield when our loved one succumbed to cancer and went to be with the Lord. Faith is our shield when we fully recover and are cured of cancer, but we don't want to go back to living in our former darkness, taking for granted the breath in our lungs. Faith is our shield against the "flaming arrows," the lies of the evil one. He is the father of lies (John 8:44), prowling around like a lion (1 Peter 5:8), seeking to destroy our faith. Faith is our shield. Faith is how we defend our souls, by God's grace.

Take hold of your eternal life in Christ Jesus

The promise of eternal life is an astounding hope. Nothing pushes down fear more than the Holy Spirit reminding us of our certain salvation in Jesus, the new bodies we'll receive, and the joy we'll have forever in His presence. Paul calls us to "take hold" of this promise of eternal life. We are to treasure it. We are to meditate on it. We are to let this hope drive away fear, knowing death is defeated and the King is alive, and as a result death has no power over us. True, we may die, but in less than one millisecond thereafter, faster than a blink of the eye, we will be raised and our spirit will be with Jesus forever. It's in this sense that we actually never die, despite our bodies dying. But *we* never die. Our souls never stop existing. This is an astounding hope that drives away fear. Take hold of it, my brothers, my sisters, my wife, my children, and all who read this, and be encouraged. Nothing truly bad can happen to us, for even the worst thing that ever happens to us can only make us stronger, better, and more joyful.

Prayer to the Lord

Lord Jesus, help me to fight the good fight of faith. Help me to believe your promises and walk in righteousness, not giving the enemy any opportunity. Help me to always be ready to share the gospel, the good news about the hope that I have in Christ Jesus, with anybody willing to listen. Be my shield, oh Lord. Protect me from doubt, from fear, from sullenness. Fight the battle for me, Lord, for my strength is insufficient, but your strength drives out all fear in me. I know I can do all things through Christ who strengthens me, even walk through the valley of the shadow of this death, for you are with me, and you will never leave me. I will be with you forever, Lord. Hallelujah!

In Jesus' name, Amen.

Question to Consider

Why is it a surprise to many that faith is a fight? In what areas of faith have you stopped fighting and need to pick up the armor of God and resume?

30 Days of Hope for Cancer Sufferers from Philippians

I've always been drawn toward the book of Philippians. My name brought me to it as a child (my full name is Phillip but most call me Phil, except my mother, of course). And now I see the providence of God in my name, chosen by my parents but designed to bring me back to the foundational truths and promises of God that are uniquely capable of helping me to persevere through this suffering with joy.

The Scriptures are always a great source of strength, of course, regardless of the name of the reader:

> For the word of God is alive and active. Sharper than any double-edged sword, it penetrates even to dividing soul and spirit, joints and marrow; it judges the thoughts and attitudes of the heart. (Hebrews 4:12)

Philippians in particular seems to be written for the encouragement of the sufferer, and I was personally strengthened mightily by journaling through it during the early days of my cancer battle. I recommend reading the entire book from beginning to end as often as you can.

In the following pages I'll be commenting on each chapter as a whole, then pulling out key verses that encourage the cancer sufferer and those who walk alongside a cancer sufferer. I think you'll agree with me that Paul was well acquainted with suffering himself and has much to offer the rest of us.

Day 31

The Good Work of God

Philippians 1

In this chapter we see Paul's relentless conviction that even despite suffering, God is doing a "good work" in us. God will carry us throughout the work, and God will bring the good work to completion at the appropriate time. This is for the glory of God and for our joy.

It is also for the joy of others, as our hope in Christ Jesus is a bright light to the world. Paul says as much, that his own suffering is for the sake of the spread of the gospel to the world, and he is happy to suffer for the sake of the gospel.

Paul goes even so far as to say that it would be better for him to die and be with Christ, yet for the sake of the gospel he wants to live. Often, we want to live for our own sakes and for fear of death. But Paul shows us a better way; he demonstrates utter contentment in the face of death and yet prays for life for the sake of *others*.

Here we see Paul's total mastery over fear. Fear has no power over him. To die is to be with Christ, and to live is to live for Christ. May it be so for us, too.

Take some time to read the whole chapter in this entry, and then we'll look closer at some parts of it in the ones after.

Philippians 1

1 Paul and Timothy, servants of Christ Jesus: To all the saints in Christ Jesus who are in Philippi, including the overseers and deacons.

2 Grace to you and peace from God our Father and the Lord Jesus Christ.

Thanksgiving and Prayer

3 I give thanks to my God for every remembrance of you, 4 always praying with joy for all of you in my every prayer, 5 be-

cause of your partnership in the gospel from the first day until now. 6 I am sure of this, that he who started a good work in you will carry it on to completion until the day of Christ Jesus. 7 Indeed, it is right for me to think this way about all of you, because I have you in my heart, and you are all partners with me in grace, both in my imprisonment and in the defense and confirmation of the gospel. 8 For God is my witness, how deeply I miss all of you with the affection of Christ Jesus. 9 And I pray this: that your love will keep on growing in knowledge and every kind of discernment, 10 so that you may approve the things that are superior and may be pure and blameless in the day of Christ, 11 filled with the fruit of righteousness that comes through Jesus Christ to the glory and praise of God.

Advance of the Gospel

12 Now I want you to know, brothers and sisters, that what has happened to me has actually advanced the gospel, 13 so that it has become known throughout the whole imperial guard, and to everyone else, that my imprisonment is because I am in Christ. 14 Most of the brothers have gained confidence in the Lord from my imprisonment and dare even more to speak the word fearlessly. 15 To be sure, some preach Christ out of envy and rivalry, but others out of good will. 16 These preach out of love, knowing that I am appointed for the defense of the gospel; 17 the others proclaim Christ out of selfish ambition, not sincerely, thinking that they will cause me trouble in my imprisonment. 18 What does it matter? Only that in every way, whether from false motives or true, Christ is proclaimed, and in this I rejoice. Yes, and I will continue to rejoice 19 because I know this will lead to my salvation[e] through your prayers and help from the Spirit of Jesus Christ. 20 My eager expectation and hope is that I will not be ashamed about anything, but that now as always, with all courage, Christ will be highly honored in my body, whether by life or by death.

Living Is Christ

21 For me, to live is Christ and to die is gain. 22 Now if I live on in the flesh, this means fruitful work for me; and I don't know which one I should choose. 23 I am torn between the two. I long to depart and be with Christ—which is far better— 24 but to remain in the flesh is more necessary for your sake. 25 Since I

*am persuaded of this, I know that I will remain and continue with all of you for your progress and joy in the faith, **26** so that, because of my coming to you again, your boasting in Christ Jesus may abound.*

***27** Just one thing: As citizens of heaven, live your life worthy of the gospel of Christ. Then, whether I come and see you or am absent, I will hear about you that you are standing firm in one spirit, in one accord, contending together for the faith of the gospel, **28** not being frightened in any way by your opponents. This is a sign of destruction for them, but of your salvation—and this is from God. **29** For it has been granted to you on Christ's behalf not only to believe in him, but also to suffer for him, **30** since you are engaged in the same struggle that you saw I had and now hear that I have.*

Prayer to the Lord

Oh Lord, give me eyes to see your glory and ears to hear and perceive your truth, so that I would live each and every day unto you without fear.

In Jesus' name, Amen.

Question to Consider

What and whom has God called you to live for? What and whom have you been living for?

Day 32

His Work Will Not Fail

Philippians 1:6

I am sure of this, that he who started a good work in you will carry it on to completion until the day of Christ Jesus.

There is too much truth in this short verse for me to even scratch the surface. It gives me *great* hope! Hope for my present health situation, hope for my wife, hope for my children. Hope for you.

My greatest fear is not death, for death will only make me stronger, better...more joyful. My greatest fear is actually for my wife and children. Who will care for them? As a father it's hard to contemplate not being around to care for my kids. But this verse tells me who will. God will.

God is doing a great work in all those who are in Christ Jesus. Aren't you so thankful for Jesus? Thankful for the price he paid on the cross? Thankful for his love? Thankful for his sovereignty over our lives? This verse tells us that he has a plan. He began a good work, He will carry us, he will complete the work he began, and a day will come when we see his Glory fully.

Here are some further observations about the verse:

God started the work

The work is *his*, and his alone. Our lives our his. It's reassuring to me to know with confidence that my salvation is in God's hands, not mine. This reminds me of Ephesians 2:8-10:

> For you are saved by grace through faith, and this

is not from yourselves; it is God's gift—not from works, so that no one can boast. For we are his workmanship, created in Christ Jesus for good works, which God prepared ahead of time for us to do.

This work of salvation is God's. All we need to do is believe in him and what he's done for us.

It's a good work

Can tragedy be "good"? Yes. Can suffering be "good"? Yes. Can cancer be a "gift"? Yes. I think the book of Philippians shows us how it can.

God uses such things to turn our eyes upon Jesus, to re-focus our lives on the things that truly matter. I wouldn't be writing this meditation if suffering hadn't forced me to gaze upon Jesus. Can you know all the ways God can use suffering in your life? No, he has 1,000 purposes for everything He does in and through you. But you can see some of them, by the Word and the Spirit.

Whether I live for only one year, or 40 more, what I know beyond a shadow of doubt is that I'm a new man. I will forever keep my eyes fixed on Jesus. I will never again shy away from sharing the gospel, from ministering the good news to those around me. And for that, I've been given the gifts of joy, hope, and peace in God, even while simultaneously harboring a tumor in my esophagus. What a miracle that is! God is doing a miracle in you, too—be patient to see it unfold.

God will complete the work

I don't have to worry about God's plan failing. Even if I were to die of cancer, does that mean God's plan failed? *No!* I need to remember that all of God's work in me is good.

We will all die one day. This creation was subjected to futility because of sin (Romans 8:20-23). But death has no sting for it is the arrival of our salvation, our entry into the heavenly gates, where we'll worship Jesus face to face.

Whatever God starts, he completes. Each of us in Christ is being used by God for some good purpose for his glory and our joy. God has a plan for each of us. God has a plan for me. God has a plan for you. A good plan. And he will carry out those plans until they are complete.

A "day" is coming

The completion of God's plan for our lives brings about the fullness of our joy, and God's glory, forevermore.

Need I fear for my health? No. Need I fear for my wife and children? No. Because God has a plan for me and for them. That plan *will* be completed. And that completion is our joy forevermore.

That "day" is coming—sooner or later, it will come. Hallelujah!

This is an astonishing hope. New bodies. New life. Being with Jesus in person. Forever. We long for this.

> Not only that, but we ourselves who have the Spirit as the firstfruits—we also groan within ourselves, eagerly waiting for adoption, the redemption of our bodies. (Romans 8:23)

We groan for the "day of Christ Jesus" to come. This world is filled with groaning. Our bodies fail. We get tumors. We suffer. We groan. But we have hope. We have hope for adoption! We have hope for redemption of these broken bodies! We *eagerly* wait!

The day of Christ Jesus is our hope, our confidence, our firm foundation. If we keep our eyes on Jesus, eager for that day, we will not stray off the path of life and righteousness. We will not lose our hope or our confidence. If we keep our eyes on Jesus we cannot be shaken, no matter what happens to us. No matter the diagnosis. Praise be to God in Christ Jesus!

Prayer to the Lord

Oh Lord, help me to see a glimmer of your pur-

poses for me in cancer. Cancer feels like an awful, terrible thing. How can it be good, Lord? Indeed, cancer is a great evil, and yet I know you can turn it for my good. I know that you, Lord, are doing a thousand things I cannot see in and through my cancer. Help me to trust in your plans for me, oh God. Help me to commit to walking in faithfulness during this challenging time, as I know you are unceasingly faithful to me, oh Lord. Hold me with your righteous right hand.

In Jesus' name, Amen.

Question to Consider

What have you seen that you know that is "good" coming from something challenging, in your life or in another person's?

Day 33

Prayers for my Wife and Children

Philippians 1:9-11

*And I pray this: that your love will keep on grow-
ing in knowledge and every kind of discernment,
so that you may approve the things that are
superior and may be pure and blameless in the
day of Christ, filled with the fruit of righteousness that comes through Jesus Christ to the
glory and praise of God.*

These verses speak to my heart for my wife and children...to
my deepest desires for them. My prayer is that, every day I
draw breath, I will encourage them toward the truths found in
these verses. I especially pray that my children would grow to
be men and women of God, firmly rooted in Him and in His
purposes, so that their lives would be filled with true hope,
true meaning, and true joy.

During the editing process of this book I nearly deleted this
chapter. It seemed too personal, because I am addressing my
wife and children directly. However, perhaps you too are a
spouse or parent who has cancer. Perhaps these meditations
are not mine alone as I had feared. My hope in leaving them in
the book is that even if you are not a spouse or parent, you can
see that our work here on earth is not done. At the very least,
our work of prayer over those we love can be a powerful legacy.

I see six requests in these verses that I am praying over my
wife and children. And because this entry is all about prayer, I
will give an example of how to pray for each one.

That your love would keep growing

The love of God is unfathomable. God loves you more than you can know. And because He first loved us, we can properly love others.

As I wrestled with my cancer diagnosis, I felt the love of those around me. The hands and feet of Christ at our church have moved me mightily. Their love, combined with God's love—in fact, God's love shown through them—is such a comfort. My prayer is you would grow in your love for others so that when the opportunity comes, you too can love those around you, lift them up, pray for them, and comfort them in their need. The quantity and quality of your love for others is an appropriate way to measure your life. Money, success, sex, etc. fail to create lasting meaning in life. But in love you will find eternal pleasures forevermore.

Prayer to the Lord

> *Lord Jesus, make the love in my wife and child-ren grow and abound for their God and those around them. Make them to know fully the love of God in Christ Jesus for them, so that they would have this solid rock on which to stand, and never be shaken. May their love overflow onto those around them, ministering the gospel and mercy. May they be the hands and feet of Christ to others as I have blessedly received during my ordeal.*
>
> *In Jesus' name, Amen.*

That your love would grow in knowledge and discernment

"Love" is a somewhat abstract term. Influencers throw it a-round all the time. I hope you will separate the world's "love" from God's love in your mind. They are two different things. God loved you so much that he sent his son Jesus to die for you, so that if you believe in him you will have eternal life. That's real love. God almighty, all powerful, humiliated himself—for *you*! My prayer is that you would know this true love and that you would live it.

Prayer to the Lord

> *Lord Jesus, make the love in my wife and children grow in knowledge and discernment of your true love. May they know the true love of God, not the superficial love of the world. May they discern your good will for them. May they discern the riches and depth of your love for them, so that they too can love those around them well.*
>
> *In Jesus' name, Amen.*

That you will know what is most important in life

The world has a lot to offer you. Fame, influence, popularity, sex, pleasures, wealth. I can tell you now beyond any doubt, in the face of cancer, what is actually important. *None* of those things have any influence on me now. For too long they did, and I fear that I wasted years that could have been spent ministering the gospel to you, loving you better.

But this is my prayer for you. Don't wait for cancer to awaken you to what is superior. Pursue the Lord *today*. Seek first the kingdom of God. When calamity strikes, all you have left is Jesus.

It reminds me of this line from the old hymn: "On Christ, the solid Rock, I stand; all other ground is sinking sand."

Knowing Jesus is superior to all worldly pleasures. As Paul said in Philippians 3:8, "Indeed, I count everything as loss because of the surpassing worth of knowing Christ Jesus my Lord. For his sake I have suffered the loss of all things and count them as rubbish, in order that I may gain Christ".

Prayer to the Lord

> *Lord Jesus, make my wife and children know the*

*surpassing worth of knowing you! May they for-
sake all worldly pleasures, enjoying your good
gifts, but not putting their hope in them. May they
wholly trust in Jesus' name. May their hope in
this world be built on nothing less than Jesus'
blood and righteousness!*

In Jesus' name, Amen.

That you may be blameless in the day of Christ

I want nothing more than your salvation and to do the will of
my Father in heaven. And if that means leaving a legacy of faith-
filled cancer, then so be it.

Know how much I love you! Feel it! I love you more than I
love myself. But I love Jesus even more, and it's for your sake
and God's glory that I do.

Someday you will understand this. Christ be praised!
When all other hopes fail, Jesus is the solid rock. Believe in him
and take hold of your salvation in Christ Jesus, from which
your hope is found!

Prayer to the Lord

*Lord Jesus, bless my wife and children with the
greatest gift you could ever give them—yourself.
May they believe in the name of Jesus and be
saved. May they spend eternity with you in heav-
en. May they taste the sweet love of Jesus for
them. May they savor you and worship you forever. For you, God, are good. May they come to
know and love your goodness for them.*

In Jesus' name, Amen.

That you will be filled with righteousness

I have discovered that the sweetest feeling someone can experience here on earth is to be filled with the Holy Spirit of God, who delivers righteousness to us by the blood of Jesus.

The utter foolishness of sin has become shockingly clear to me. Old vices that once tempted my soul continuously are nothing but rubbish.

My clarity of purpose was firmly established; to give God glory with every breath he gives me. While sorrowful at my diagnosis, I was yet filled with Joy. Sorrowful, yet joyful! How God works in our lives is an amazing mystery, isn't it?

Prayer to the Lord

> *Lord Jesus, help my wife and children to continually walk in righteousness, being filled with the Spirit, ready for every good work. May they taste the sweetness of your Spirit. May sin be an anathema to them! May their righteousness exceed that of the scribes and Pharisees (Matthew 5:20), because they know that their righteousness is actually Christ's, given to them—not as a result of their good deeds, so that they cannot boast (Ephesians 2:8-9). Help them to know and believe that their righteousness is the free gift of God for them!*
>
> *In Jesus' name, Amen.*

That your life would glorify God

Why are we here on this earth? Why were we born? Why is there even an earth, a sun, or a universe? The Bible says "The heavens declare the glory of God, and the expanse proclaims the work of his hands" (Psalm 19:1). The Bible gives us a reason why we're here, why anything is here. All this is here to declare the glory of God!

Atheists believe it was all a random accident. But how can something come to exist out of nothing? Where did that infinitely dense "speck" from? What caused it to "big bang" if it was not God who spoke and caused the matter to explode forth?

Honestly, the "faith" of the unbeliever exceeds that of the Christian, despite their denials of faith. They, too, must believe in some incredible things, or at least try to ignore some key questions.

The answer the Bible gives us is clear: we are here to glorify God. To my dear wife, children, and friends, I say: Know this and you will know your purpose. Unfortunately, it took staring cancer in the face for me to have such clarity of purpose. I pray it won't be that way for you.

Prayer to the Lord

Lord Jesus, may you be glorified in the lives of my wife and children. May they know you and your glory. Show them your glory, oh God! May their purpose in life, their mission, their aspirations, their affections, their hopes, and their dreams be for your glory. It's for their joy that I pray this.

In Jesus' name, Amen.

Question to Consider

Is there anything in your heart or life that the Lord is calling you to repent from or to let go of? How can you glorify him in those areas of your life?

Day 34

What Happened to Me is "Good"

Philippians 1:12

Now I want you to know, brothers and sisters, that what has happened to me has actually advanced the gospel.

When Paul wrote that verse, he was suffering an unjust imprisonment, which he says, in a way, was actually a good thing that happened to him. This fits with what he says in Romans 8:28:

We know that all things work together for the good of those who love God, who are called according to his purpose.

How could Paul's imprisonment be a good thing? How could cancer be a good thing? It's an important and difficult question, but I can think of a few reasons cancer has been good for me. Take this verse as an example:

We felt that we had received the sentence of death. But that was to make us rely not on ourselves but on God who raises the dead. (2 Corinthians 1:8-9)

Since I received my "sentence of death," I have had to rely more on God than ever before in my life. And that is a good thing. I am in communion with the Holy Spirit. I'm in community with believers encouraging me. I'm continually, all day, every day, turning to Jesus for strength. And as a result, hope is abounding. It's a good thing to have learned to rely on Jesus, our one and only sure foundation.

In a similar way, cancer can be "good" for my family as well, though it's hard to watch my children learn this lesson. When you're 12, or even 16, "faith" is usually a rather abstract idea. But for my children, by necessity, it has become a practice, a way of life. That is my hope and joy for them, that they would know the Lord and be brought close to Him. I know my suffering is for the strengthening of their faith as well, and that gives me great courage to endure it.

As a father, I would gladly take a bullet for any of my children...no hesitation. So should I not endure this hardship for their sake as well? It's a wonderful opportunity for them to see their father walking with the Lord, to see faith in action. May God give me strength to lead my family in the Word and in truth during this trial, that they may see the hope set before me and take hold of that same hope for themselves, a hope in Christ Jesus.

After we told the kids about my cancer, I was sitting with my son Henry and he asked, "Why doesn't God just kill Satan?" It was such an honest question. Why doesn't God just take away all the suffering in this world? The answer lies in God Himself.

God is...God. Matchless. Powerful. Almighty.

Yes, He could take Satan out, and he will do just that at the proper time.

God could have just eliminated our will and choices and forced all of us to worship him. He could have made us into little robots that sing his praises for eternity apart from any desire on our part. But the god receiving that kind of praise would not be as great as our God.

Our God created us for his glory, to be sure. But God is most glorified in us when we are most satisfied in Him (see the great book *Desiring God* by John Piper for more on this).

What gives God more glory—a robot pre-programmed to worship with no choice in the matter or a man who is afflicted with cancer yet willingly chooses to trust in a good God who loves him? It's an amazing thing to be filled with the Holy Spirit during a harsh trial...to be sorrowful, yet joyful. This gives God a lot of glory, and as a result, even a great evil such as cancer can be reframed as "good."

Paul says that his affliction was good because the gospel was advanced because of it. This means the gospel would not have advanced as much if it weren't for the affliction, so Paul was glad the affliction came.

I can say this is true for me as well. The gospel has advanced in my home. I will never again abate my zeal for the salvation of my children. The gospel has advanced in my work. I will not hesitate to share where my hope is during this trial. The gospel has advanced in my community. I will shout it from the rooftops; I will not muffle my voice when walking past neighbors, but will instead extol Jesus in a loud voice!

The gospel advances in a million ways that you cannot yet fathom and may never know. You don't always see God working, but he is. You need to trust that God will bring about "good to those who love God" even if you cannot see how or why.

In Genesis 50:20, Joseph's brothers had done a great evil against Joseph, but Joseph saw how God used that evil for good purposes:

> You planned evil against me; God planned it for good to bring about the present result—the survival of many people.

Prayer to the Lord

> *Father God, use me for your purposes. Use my cancer, oh God, for the spread of your gospel. Help me to boldly share the hope I have in Christ Jesus with those whom you put in my path. Help me, oh Lord, not to be ashamed of the gospel, for it is the power of God to everyone being saved.*
>
> *In Jesus' name, Amen.*

Question to Consider

> *Who in your life needs to hear the gospel, and how is the Lord leading you to share it with them?*

Day 35

To Live is Christ, to Die is Gain

Philippians 1:14, 20-21

Most of the brothers have gained confidence in the Lord from my imprisonment and dare even more to speak the word fearlessly.... My eager expectation and hope is that I will not be ashamed about anything, but that now as always, with all courage, Christ will be highly honored in my body, whether by life or by death. For me, to live is Christ and to die is gain.

In the Old Testament, God had his people raise up a temple where the people of God were to worship him, offering sacrifices for their atonement and the removal of their sins. As with much of the Old Testament, these physical things symbolized and foreshadowed spiritual things. Jesus was the ultimate, perfect sacrifice—the Lamb provided by God to be the final sacrifice for our sins. Thereafter, a physical temple was no longer necessary. The price was paid, forever! Sacrifices were no longer needed.

But the temple wasn't just for sacrifices; the "Most Holy Place" within the temple was the place where the people of God met with God.

So where do we meet with God now? Paul tells us in 1 Corinthians 6:19:

> Don't you know that your body is a temple of the Holy Spirit who is in you, whom you have from God? You are not your own.

We are the temple of God; the Spirit of God lives within us. We can meet with God even when we are alone—in prayer and meditation on God's Word.

Paul's words in I Corinthians 6:19 imply that our bodies are important, and in Philippians 1 we see Paul's desire to honor Christ in his body, whether by death or life. Below are four meditations from these passages on how our bodies, in death or life, can be used to glorify God:

Your suffering can inspire confidence and fearlessness in others

We can't always know the ways of God or all the ends of His good plan for us. He plans for our good but also for the good of others. God's plan for Paul included both, according to Philippians 1.

I doubt that Paul wanted to be imprisoned, but he did desire the will of God. And this is a reminder of how the will of God can be working in ways we don't always expect. God was building up the church through Paul's suffering. God was turning terrible circumstances for not just Paul's good, but for the good of others too. This is similar to Joseph's enslavement in Genesis—an evil that was turned not just for Joseph's good, but for the salvation of millions of people. God is doing a thousand things in and through our lives that we may never realize until the "big picture" of God's plans are finally revealed to us in heaven.

You should not be ashamed

I think there's a connection between fearlessness in verse 14 and shame in verse 20. This is not to say fear is shameful, *per se*. But I am reminded that Paul also mentions shame in Romans 1:16:

> For I am not ashamed of the gospel, because it is the power of God for salvation to everyone who believes.

The brothers and sisters in Philippi were not ashamed of the gospel. In fact, they were fearless in the sharing of it. Their fearlessness was born, apparently, from the example of Paul and his imprisonment.

In Philippians 1 Paul shares his own intentions to not be ashamed of anything. What could he possibly be ashamed of? I'm guessing, based on the context, that he may have been concerned that the fear he felt in his present situation might manifest as shame. I feel that fear as well.

I don't want my children to see their father succumb to fear, or be defined by fear. It would be shameful if their last memories are of me cowering in the face of death, having lost all hope in the saving grace of God in Christ Jesus and not experiencing the peace of God. I expect good and bad feelings to ebb and flow in me, of course, but I want my children to see in me a genuine hope in the relentless love of God for me and the ultimate redemption of my body, either in the healing of my cancer or in the reception of a new body in heaven.

I resonate with Paul in that I too do not want to be ashamed of anything. My desire is that God would be glorified in my body. With the courage supplied by Jesus, I know this is possible.

You can do all things through Christ who strengthens you. You can walk with cancer, sorrowful to be sure, but yet always rejoicing in God's promises for you. This will give you the strength to leave a legacy of hope and courage to your family and those around you. You need not be ashamed of anything.

Honoring Christ in your body is not contingent on living...or dying

Paul didn't give God any ultimatums. He didn't say "I'll live for you if...." No, in verse 20 he says, "My eager expectation and hope [is that] Christ will be highly honored in my body, whether by life or by death."

Christ *will* be highly exalted in Paul, regardless of whether he dies or not. That is Paul's expectation and hope. He is more concerned with the glory of God than living or dying.

Do you want to be healed more than you want Christ glorified? Of course not—no true believer would say that. And yet a desire for healing above all else is a natural human response.

Satan and the flesh don't want Christ glorified in this trial. Satan wants fear to take root and make healing an idol in your heart.

But you know that is folly. Someday, whether tomorrow or 40 years from now, you will die. Why cling to something that is certain to fail you eventually? The only sure hope is for life eternal with Jesus. "The one who loves his life will lose it," he said, "and the one who hates his life in this world will keep it for eternal life" (John 12:25).

To live is Christ, to die is gain

Paul had an astonishing hope in Christ Jesus. The worst thing that could ever happen to him, he considered *gain*.

Fear of death is a natural response for all of us. I'd be lying if I didn't acknowledge the many tears I've shed because of this fear. But God didn't give Paul, nor me, nor you, a spirit of fear. He gave us a spirit of power in Christ Jesus, as Paul tells us in 2 Timothy 1:7.

By this spirit of power, you can stand firm in the face of death and know that to die is your gain. Death can only make you stronger. Death can only bring you the fullness of joy in the presence of Jesus. Death can only *restore* your body, not destroy it.

After I finished writing this entry and praying about it, the following song came up on my playlist. Read the words and be reminded of the spirit of power we have in Christ Jesus to conquer any fear of death that we may be harboring. In Jesus, death is defeated. Look to him!

Break Every Chain
(written by Will Reagan in 2009)

There is power in the name of Jesus
There is power in the name of Jesus
There is power in the name of Jesus
To break every chain
To break every chain
All sufficient sacrifice

So freely given
Such a price
Bought our redemption
Heaven's gates
Swing wide
We believe

There is power in the name of Jesus...
To break every chain!

Blessed to God
Oh Hallelujah
Give him glory

Prayer to the Lord

Lord God, help me to be fearless in sharing the hope I have in Christ Jesus with all those you put in my path. Help me not to be ashamed of the gospel, for it's your power to save. Likewise, help me to be fearless in cancer. Be honored in my body, oh Lord, whether in living or dying. Help me to live for Christ each and every day you give me, and when the time comes for me to depart, help me not to fear but rather to rejoice with expectation of the hope set before me in the eternal life you have promised me.

In Jesus' name, Amen.

Question to Consider

In what ways might the Lord be calling you to live for Christ and not for yourself?

Day 36

To Be or Not to Be

Philippians 1:22-26

Now if I live on in the flesh, this means fruitful work for me; and I don't know which one I should choose. I am torn between the two. I long to depart and be with Christ—which is far better— but to remain in the flesh is more necessary for your sake. Since I am persuaded of this, I know that I will remain and continue with all of you for your progress and joy in the faith, so that, because of my coming to you again, your boasting in Christ Jesus may abound.

As I mentioned before, John Piper says in his book *Desiring God* that "God is most glorified in us when we are most satisfied in Him." God is most glorified in my dying when I die fully hopeful in the promises of God for me. God is most glorified in my healing when I know that God is... God(!), and "from him and through him and to him are all things" (Romans 11:36). The healing is from Him. The healing is through him. The healing is *for* Him more than it is for me.

Following are three key takeaways from these verses in Philippians 1 for those walking through cancer.

To live means fruitful work

Paul clearly saw living as an opportunity for fruitful work for the glory of Christ. We see this in verse 22, but also in verses 24-25. His reason to "remain and continue" was *their* progress and joy (verse 25).

Paul's purpose for living was not for his benefit but rather for the benefit of others. He said "to live is Christ," and living for Christ by definition means fruitful work in which we serve others.

Why I want to live is important for me in my cancer journey. I want to live, not for my sake alone, but for the sake of those God has put around me to bless.

I know there is no going back to my old way of life. I know going forward that I'm a new man with a new clarity of purpose—the building up of the saints, especially my wife and children, for their "progress and joy." Like Paul, that's why I want to live.

It's normal for Christians to be conflicted about life and death

It was difficult for Paul to determine whether he preferred to die and be with Jesus, or to live and work toward the progress and joy of the church. We learn from this that it's not unusual or necessarily wrong for a Christian to have this kind of struggle. The fact is, to die and be with Christ *is* actually preferable. Paul tells us, "I long to depart and be with Christ—which is far better."

Romans 8:23 also tells us that those who know Christ long to depart and be with Jesus forever:

> Not only that, but we ourselves who have the Spirit as the firstfruits—we also groan within ourselves, eagerly waiting for adoption, the redemption of our bodies.

But despite all this, Paul says that he will "remain and continue" in this life. And indeed he did. He lived for several more years after he wrote this letter to the Philippians. God's plan for Paul was not complete—he had years of fruitful work left, and the impact those years had on the world is incalculable. That's our God. You will not depart this world until his plan for you has been accomplished.

Another good motive for remaining is the glory of God

In verse 26 Paul says that he will remain alive for a time, not because of his own desire to live but so that there could be more "boasting in Jesus Christ." He would remain, because in doing so God would receive the most glory.

I don't know yet what God will do with my cancer. Will God be given more glory in my healing, or in my death? God knows, and I'll submit to His purposes.

There is great freedom from fear in wanting God's glory more than my healing. I will die eventually. It may be one year from now, or 40. I cannot know. What I do know is that I cannot put my hope in healing. No matter what, whether sooner or later, any healing will become undone. My body will fail me. Why put my hope in healing? It is temporary at best.

This is not to say I don't pray earnestly, with desperation even, for healing. I do! But my hope is not in it. My hope is in Jesus, and my desire is the glory of God, for the glory of God is everlasting. The presence of the Holy Spirit will never fail. It's a sure hope.

The healing I will receive, either in this life or the next, is congruent with the glory of God because it's *God* who does the healing. God getting the glory is the natural outcome of my healing.

I cannot give the glory for healing to doctors or medicines, and I cannot give the glory for healing to myself, because the reality is that many are not healed from cancer. The glory goes to God because he at times uses healing, as he also uses dying, to reveal his Divine attributes (John 9:3, Romans 9:17-24).

God uses doctors, medicines, and healthy habits to bring about healing, and we should be deeply thankful for them. But we don't put our hope in them. We put our hope in God for our healing. And what we desire even more is that God would be glorified in us. Our desire is that "boasting may abound in Christ Jesus." We will boast in God!

Prayer to the Lord

> *Lord Jesus, thank you for revealing yourself to me. Thank you for giving me confidence in the salvation that I have by believing in you, so that*

whether in life or death I will praise you in the great hope of living forever for your glory. Grant me fruitful work in my days on earth. Give me strength to set my hand to the plow and toil for the progress and joy of those around me. With each day you give me, Lord, may I strive for the gospel and for your glory. I can do this only through the strength you supply.

In Jesus' name, Amen.

Question to Consider

Whose "progress and joy" is the Lord calling you to live for in the days you have left on this earth?

Day 37

A Worthy Life

Philippians 1:27

Just one thing: As citizens of heaven, live your life worthy of the gospel of Christ.

My most urgent prayers for my children are that they would know *who* they are, and *whose* they are. I pray that they would find their identity in Christ Jesus, that they would know they are children of God, and that they would live like their citizenship is in heaven, not on earth.

It's so easy for us to become a case of "mistaken identity." For too long my identity was based on my work. Then in recent years I found my identity in losing weight and getting stronger in the gym, in financial success, in things like fancy cars and status. In the face of cancer all these things now seem like rubbish. It's unfortunate that it took cancer to awaken me from my slumber, but it's better to awaken than not to.

My children are teenagers in the throes of trying to figure out who they are. And yet, the process of working on your identity really never stops. I'm in my 40s and am still learning important lessons about this, now more than ever.

My prayer for them is that it would not require a tragedy for them to know their worth in Christ Jesus. I have often prayed for them that they would make good choices. I've prayed against sullenness, anger, snottiness, and other forms of misbehaving. But Paul's words in this verse imply that we can only "live worthy" when we are frequently reminded of our worth in Christ. Our behaviors flow out of what we find our identity in.

So my prayers against sullenness, anger, snottiness, etc. will continue. But more urgently my prayer is that they would know who they are, and whose they are. I pray this for you too.

Pray this for yourself. Pray that you would be rooted in Christ, that your identity would be in him.

Prayer to the Lord

Lord Jesus, open my eyes to see your glory! Open my heart to know the love of God for me! May my identity be found in Jesus! May I see myself as a citizen of heaven, and through that knowledge walk in this world worthy of that citizenship. May my identity be so rooted in Jesus that sin would have no ground from which to take root in my heart.

In Jesus' name, Amen.

Question to Consider

What does "live worthy of the gospel" mean for your life? What is God's call on you for the gospel?

Day 38

More About Fear

Philippians 1:27-29

I will hear about you...not being frightened in any way by your opponents. This is a sign of destruction for them, but of your salvation—and this is from God. For it has been granted to you on Christ's behalf not only to believe in him, but also to suffer for him.

Much of the book of Philippians is about suffering, and much of Chapter 1 is about fear. This tells us that fear is a natural response when we suffer, and it's okay to feel fear ebb and flow. But it's not okay to live in fear, to linger in it, to let it take root in our hearts. So in these final verses of Chapter 1, Paul gives us some powerful ammunition to use against fear.

First, he tells us that *courage is a sign of our salvation.* Courage in the face of fear is both an inward and outward sign from God. Inwardly, we ourselves are comforted, knowing the truths that God is with us and will never forsake us (Deuteronomy 31:6). Outwardly, our courage is a sign for others that God is real and dwelling in us.

By the grace that God supplies, don't waste cancer by allowing others to see fear as the foundation or driving force of your emotional state, whether it's your battle or a loved one's. Instead let your hope in Christ abound to the benefit of others, so that they may see your faith in the midst of fear and know that Jesus is alive. This will be a sign from God for the building up of faith in others and, to borrow Paul's words from earlier in Chapter 1, a fruitful work for their progress and joy.

Paul also tells us that *suffering is a gift of God.* "The problem of evil" is a question for the ages. Volumes of books have been written on it. Atheists use it to say there can be no God, but we believers see the mystery of how God does not cause evil, but he does turn evil for our good and his glory.

Suffering has been "granted to you" so that you would learn not to rely on yourself but on God. Remember what Paul says in 2 Corinthians 1:8-9:

> We do not want you to be unaware, brothers, of the affliction we experienced in Asia.... We felt that we had received the sentence of death. But that was to make us rely not on ourselves but on God who raises the dead.

Paul felt that he had received the sentence of death. He was walking through deep waters. And yet, Paul knew that a great good was taking shape through his suffering. He was learning to rely on God and not himself.

The church itself was built on the suffering of the saints. Countless thousands died, and still die today, because of the persecution of Christians. One would have thought the robustness of such persecution in the early days of the church would have snuffed out the church altogether. But quite the opposite happened, and still happens today.

As we already learned, courage in the face of death is a powerful sign to unbelievers. Suffering is an opportunity to show the world what we believe to be true and how much we really believe it. Many have been saved because they witness the incomprehensible faith of those dying for Jesus. Death is a bad thing—it's called our "enemy" in 1 Corinthians 15:26—but God uses it to bring about the salvation of the lost. The best example of this, of course, is the death of Jesus on the cross.

It's for the sake of the glory of Christ that we suffer. It's for the sake of the salvation of many that we suffer. It's because of this that we can suffer with joy, knowing suffering yields fruit for the Kingdom of God. Two powerful passages in 1 Peter tell us how salvation is connected to suffering, and they are a perfect way to wrap our discussions of Philippians 1:

> Blessed be the God and Father of our Lord Jesus

Christ. Because of his great mercy he has given us new birth into a living hope through the resurrection of Jesus Christ from the dead and into an inheritance that is imperishable, undefiled, and unfading, kept in heaven for you. You are being guarded by God's power through faith for a salvation that is ready to be revealed in the last time. You rejoice in this, even though now for a short time, if necessary, you suffer grief in various trials so that the proven character of your faith—more valuable than gold which, though perishable, is refined by fire—may result in praise, glory, and honor at the revelation of Jesus Christ. Though you have not seen him, you love him; though not seeing him now, you believe in him, and you rejoice with inexpressible and glorious joy, because you are receiving the goal of your faith, the salvation of your souls. (1 Peter 1: 3-9)

Dear friends, don't be surprised when the fiery ordeal comes among you to test you, as if something unusual were happening to you. Instead, rejoice as you share in the sufferings of Christ, so that you may also rejoice with great joy when his glory is revealed. If you are ridiculed for the name of Christ, you are blessed, because the Spirit of glory and of God rests on you. Let none of you suffer as a murderer, a thief, an evildoer, or a meddler. But if anyone suffers as a Christian, let him not be ashamed but let him glorify God in having that name. For the time has come for judgment to begin with God's household, and if it begins with us, what will the outcome be for those who disobey the gospel of God? And if a righteous person is saved with difficulty, what will become of the ungodly and the sinner? So then, let those who suffer according to God's will entrust themselves to a faithful Creator while doing what is good. (1 Peter 4:12-19)

Prayer to the Lord

Lord, help me not to be afraid of this suffering I'm experiencing, for I know it is not a surprise to you. Draw near to me, oh Lord, so that I would not fear but rather endure this suffering with faith and hope.

In Jesus' name, Amen.

Question to Consider

How might God be using your suffering to bring the lost to salvation?

Day 39

Christ's Love and Ours

Philippians 2

The dominant theme in this chapter is love. We see Paul's eager desire for the love of the Philippians to grow in the service and encouragement of each other, where they would by God's grace consider others as more important than themselves.

We also see how Paul's reflecting on the humility and glory of Jesus translates into a confidence that his suffering is not in vain. Just as Christ did, Paul suffers for the building up of the church. In this we learn that our own suffering is not in vain when we allow God to use it to strengthen the faith of others.

Finally, we see the importance of community as an expression of love. Paul sent Timothy and Epaphroditus to Philippi for their comfort and encouragement, but also for his own. In this we learn the importance of supporting each other as a prime example of what love looks like.

Take some time today to read this whole chapter and then we'll look closer at some key parts of it...

Philippians 2

If, then, there is any encouragement in Christ, if any consolation of love, if any fellowship with the Spirit, if any affection and mercy, 2 make my joy complete by thinking the same way, having the same love, united in spirit, intent on one purpose. 3 Do nothing out of selfish ambition or conceit, but in humility consider others as more important than yourselves. 4 Everyone should look not to his own interests, but rather to the interests of others.

Christ's Humility and Exaltation

5 Adopt the same attitude as that of Christ Jesus, 6 who, existing in the form of God, did not consider equality with God

140

as something to be exploited. **7** Instead he emptied himself by assuming the form of a servant, taking on the likeness of humanity. And when he had come as a man, **8** he humbled himself by becoming obedient to the point of death—even to death on a cross.

9 For this reason God highly exalted him and gave him the name that is above every name, **10** so that at the name of Jesus every knee will bow—in heaven and on earth and under the earth—**11** and every tongue will confess that Jesus Christ is Lord, to the glory of God the Father.

Lights in the World

12 Therefore, my dear friends, just as you have always obeyed, so now, not only in my presence but even more in my absence, work out your own salvation with fear and trembling. **13** For it is God who is working in you both to will and to work according to his good purpose. **14** Do everything without grumbling and arguing, **15** so that you may be blameless and pure, children of God who are faultless in a crooked and perverted generation, among whom you shine like stars in the world, **16** by holding firm to the word of life. Then I can boast in the day of Christ that I didn't run or labor for nothing. **17** But even if I am poured out as a drink offering on the sacrificial service of your faith, I am glad and rejoice with all of you. **18** In the same way you should also be glad and rejoice with me.

Timothy and Epaphroditus

19 Now I hope in the Lord Jesus to send Timothy to you soon so that I too may be encouraged by news about you. **20** For I have no one else like-minded who will genuinely care about your interests; **21** all seek their own interests, not those of Jesus Christ. **22** But you know his proven character, because he has served with me in the gospel ministry like a son with a father. **23** Therefore, I hope to send him as soon as I see how things go with me. **24** I am confident in the Lord that I myself will also come soon.

25 But I considered it necessary to send you Epaphroditus—my brother, coworker, and fellow soldier, as well as your messenger and minister to my need— **26** since he has been longing for all of you and was distressed because you heard that he was sick. **27** Indeed, he was so sick that he nearly died.

However, God had mercy on him, and not only on him but also on me, so that I would not have sorrow upon sorrow. 28 For this reason, I am very eager to send him so that you may rejoice again when you see him and I may be less anxious. 29 Therefore, welcome him in the Lord with great joy and hold people like him in honor, 30 because he came close to death for the work of Christ, risking his life to make up what was lacking in your ministry to me.

Prayer to the Lord

Help me Lord to love others well, for this is your command to me, that I would love the Lord God with all my heart and love others as myself. Help love to be what people see as my most defining attribute. Work this miracle in me, oh Lord.

In Jesus' name, Amen.

Question to Consider

In what areas of your life do you wish grumbling and arguing would give way to love?

Day 40

The Interests of Others

Philippians 2:1-4

If, then, there is any encouragement in Christ, if any consolation of love, if any fellowship with the Spirit, if any affection and mercy, make my joy complete by thinking the same way, having the same love, united in spirit, intent on one purpose. Do nothing out of selfish ambition or conceit, but in humility consider others as more important than yourselves. Everyone should look not to his own interests, but rather to the interests of others.

Paul brings us back to love in these verses after a long discourse on suffering and affliction. When suffering comes, a natural response is to be self-centered, but God wants something far different for us. Let's take a closer look at what Paul says here...

Paul's joy is full in the knowledge of their love

We need to remember that Paul wrote this while being imprisoned and persecuted for his faith. His joy wasn't centered on the hope of regaining his freedom, but rather the knowledge of the love of others. He said to the Philippians, "Make my joy complete by thinking the same way, having the same love, united in spirit, intent on one purpose."

The best way I can understand this is to think of how Paul had taken on the role of a spiritual father to them. As a father with cancer, my thoughts often go to my children, who are my legacy. What I want for them more than anything is to know the love of Christ Jesus for them, and what he means by "love your neighbor as yourself" (Matthew 22:39) and "love your enemies" (Matthew 5:44).

In a similar way, as their spiritual father, Paul wanted more than anything to hear word of the love of the Philippians, for such love is the inevitable fruit of God's work in a heart. He earnestly longed for their salvation, and so he looked eagerly for their fruit.

Paul wants them to consider the interests of others as more important than their own

Paul's chief concern was the salvation of the people in Philippi, and that they would bear the fruit of love for those around them. This shows an incredible selflessness in Paul. He could have asked them to pray for his release from prison. I don't know about you, but to me that seems like the obvious thing for him to write about.

On many occasions, during my cancer struggle, I have reached out to old friends, asking them to pray for me, knowing in many cases I haven't talked with them in years. I reach out to them because I know they love me and will pray, and I know the prayers of the saints are powerful (James 5:16). However, Paul here reminds me that it's not all about me. Despite his suffering and imprisonment, his concern was for *their* situation, not his. This is quite remarkable, and a miracle of the Holy Spirit.

I'm not saying we shouldn't be concerned with our cancer and we shouldn't desire prayer and fellowship from the body of Christ, the hands and feet of Jesus—of course we should. However, even in cancer, we still should strive to consider others' interests as more important than our own.

That's what we see in Jesus dying on the cross, after all. He certainly would never have volunteered for such an agonizing death if it weren't for a deep desire for the good of others. Remember, Jesus had an opportunity to walk away; he could have saved his life on many occasions. But he didn't; he gave his life for us. For us!

Can a cancer patient similarly be marked by his or her love

for others? Paul and Jesus show us that it's possible through God who strengthens us.

I'm not sure what this looks like in your life. For me, my primary aim is for fruitful work in the gospel toward my wife and children with every day I am given. I want them to know the hope I have in Christ Jesus, and I want that for everyone else too. And yet, apart from my wife and children, considering others as more important than myself does not come naturally. That's only possible through a spiritual work in our hearts by the Holy Spirit.

Let us pray for such selflessness, for Paul commands us, *"Imitate me, as I also imitate Christ"* (1 Corinthians 11:1).

Prayer to the Lord

> *Holy Spirit, work in me so that I will not only be marked by a concern for my own healing, but even more for my concern for the salvation and love of others. Help me, despite cancer, to consider others' needs as more important than my own. I know, Lord, that only you can give me such a heart of faith, given the burden of concern I have for my health. As such, I ask in Jesus' name for your Holy Spirit to work this miracle in my heart, that I would love others more than myself, just as Jesus and Paul did.*

> *In Jesus' name, Amen.*

Question to Consider

> *Even in the midst of cancer, in what ways do you think you can still be serving others' needs?*

Day 41

Every Knee Will Bow

Philippians 2:9-11

For this reason God highly exalted him and gave him the name that is above every name, so that at the name of Jesus every knee will bow—in heaven and on earth and under the earth—and every tongue will confess that Jesus Christ is Lord, to the glory of God the Father.

The main point of the Bible is not the *recording* of historical events. Rather, the main point of the Bible is the *revealing* of the glory of God, primarily through the story of his Son Jesus Christ.

In these verses Paul reminds the Philippians of the glory of God in Jesus. The context leading up to these verses is Paul's testimony of living for Christ and his urgent desire for the people in Philippi to live for Him also. Then in Philippians 2:5-7 Paul says (my paraphrase):

> Adopt the same attitude as that of Christ Jesus, who, despite being God, emptied himself by assuming the form of a servant, taking on the likeness of humanity. He humbled himself by becoming obedient to the point of death, even death on a cross.

That's our context. The Son of God, the all-powerful creator of the universe, came down to earth as a man and humbled himself, being obedient to the will of the Father, even unto death on a cross. *Therefore*, God highly exalted him and gave him the name that is above every name (verse 9)!

The crucifixion and resurrection are the greatest revelation of the glory of God imaginable. It's actually rather incomprehensible that God...God himself!...would come to earth and die for us.

God coming to earth to rule—that is imaginable. In fact, that is what most Jews in that day were expecting. They were expecting a messiah to come as a king who would rule over them.

But an earthly rule at Jesus' first coming was not God's plan for maximizing his glory. Jesus had to suffer first, for in his suffering God was most glorified in him. The writer of Hebrews speaks to this:

> But we do see Jesus—made lower than the angels for a short time so that by God's grace he might taste death for everyone—crowned with glory and honor because he suffered death. (Hebrews 2:9)

Jesus would still be deserving of glory and honor even if he had not died for us. But oh how much we *enjoy* praising his name for his saving us. It's a joy to worship Jesus and glorify him, not just because he deserves it for who he is, but also because of our thankfulness for what he did for us. This glory on top of glory was God's purpose in sending Jesus. His purpose was for our joy, to be sure, but his main purpose was the additional, incremental, incomprehensible revealing of his glory.

We see the glory of God revealed in Jesus Christ throughout the entire Bible. The whole chapter of Isaiah 53, for example, is a prophecy of the suffering of Jesus and his glorification afterward. The New Testament is riddled with declarations about the glory of Jesus. This is what it's all about, folks. The glory of God as seen in Jesus is what life is all about.

Cancer can make me focus inward in my thoughts. I can pray for healing for my own sake. I can pray for peace for my own sake. In the depths of sorrow and fear it's hard to look past my cancer and see the glory of God in Jesus. And yet, when I do, my hope wells up because I see how God can use this great evil and turn it for my good.

He turns it for my good because God is given much glory when I credit my healing to *him*.

He turns it for my good because God is given much glory when I credit my peace to *him*.

He turns it for my good because God is given much glory when I credit my hope to *him*.

When we trust in Jesus during suffering, the angels watch and praise God for our faith.

When we trust in Jesus during suffering, our enemy Satan and his minions watch and shudder, seeing their plans for us unravel.

When we trust in Jesus during suffering, people around us see our hope in God and come to believe in Jesus because of the power of God seen in our faith—and their worship rises up anew to the glory of God.

I'll leave you with a smattering of other passages that speak to the glory of God in Jesus being revealed. Meditate on how God may use your cancer by turning it to praise from you and others...

John 2:11
Jesus did this, the first of his signs, in Cana of Galilee. He revealed his glory, and his disciples believed in him.

John 11:4
When Jesus heard it, he said, "This sickness will not end in death but is for the glory of God, so that the Son of God may be glorified through it."

John 11:40
Jesus said to her, "Didn't I tell you that if you believed you would see the glory of God?"

Acts 7:55
Stephen, full of the Holy Spirit, gazed into heaven. He saw the glory of God, and Jesus standing at the right hand of God.

2 Corinthians 4:6
For God who said, "Let light shine out of darkness," has shone in our hearts to give the light of the knowledge of God's glory in the face of Jesus Christ.

Titus 2:13
While we wait for the blessed hope, the appearing of the glory of our great God and Savior, Jesus Christ.

1 Peter 1:7
So that the proven character of your faith—more valuable than gold which, though perishable, is refined by fire—may result in praise, glory, and honor at the revelation of Jesus Christ.

1 Peter 4:11
If anyone speaks, let it be as one who speaks God's words; if anyone serves, let it be from the strength God provides, so that God may be glorified through Jesus Christ in everything. To him be the glory and the power forever and ever. Amen.

Prayer to the Lord

Lord Jesus, I worship you. You are my king and I bow before you. Thank you for revealing your glory to me through faith. Help me to glorify your name in my life.

In Jesus' name, Amen.

Question to Consider

How might God use your battle with cancer to glorify Christ Jesus? With whom can you share your hope in Jesus?

Day 42

Work Out Your Salvation

Philippians 2:12-16

*Therefore, my dear friends, just as you have al-
ways obeyed, so now, not only in my presence
but even more in my absence, work out your own
salvation with fear and trembling. For it is God
who is working in you both to will and to work
according to his good purpose. Do everything
without grumbling and arguing, so that you may
be blameless and pure, children of God who are
faultless in a crooked and perverted generation,
among whom you shine like stars in the world,
by holding firm to the word of life.*

Immediately after discussing the glory of God revealed to us in
Christ Jesus, Paul turns our attention to how therefore we
should live in the knowledge of the glory of God. Remember
this: glory first, good deeds second.

The glory of God in Christ Jesus, when it captures our
heart, changes us. We desire to walk in obedience as an overflow from having encountered his glory, having received his
grace. Whenever we talk about obedience, I think it's important to remember that we are saved by grace through faith, not
by obedience, lest we think that our good deeds have purch-
ased our salvation.

In themselves, our good deeds are only as valuable as filthy
rags (Isaiah 64:6). We should never do them in an attempt to
earn salvation, but *because* God saved us by grace through
faith in Christ (Ephesians 2:8-9). We do not trust in or rely on
our works—we trust in and rely on the work he did for us on
the cross.

As you "work out your salvation" through times of suffering, the following insights from this passage will be helpful to you...

You should not obey to please people

Paul was concerned, it seems, that the Philippians' obedience in Christ might stop now that he was no longer with him. That's not surprising; many people will act a certain way on Sunday mornings at church, and another way the rest of the week. This is because their real desire is to look good in the eyes of other people.

However, there is another possible explanation for Paul's concern. Maybe Paul simply knew that since he wasn't with them in person, his faith couldn't carry them. Being led and taught by an apostle must have been an amazing thing, so I can imagine that the people of Philippi sincerely desired to be with Paul again in person and therefore were susceptible to discouragement in his absence.

For me, these verses are a reminder that I'm in a spiritual battle whether I'm alone or with other people. Sometimes, when with other people, I put on my strong face, but then in solitude I feel depressed. I don't necessarily think this is abnormal or bad; I want people to see the hope I have in Christ Jesus. But I also want people to know that fighting for faith does have its ups and downs. Sullenness is rooted in unbelief in God's goodness for me, which is sin. Paul's words remind me to be authentic about how I'm feeling all the time so that my brothers and sisters in Christ can fight with me and for me, and not be deceived in any way about what their own trials will be like.

Having seen Jesus' glory, you can have good fear and trembling

Remember that the context for the obedience discussed in this passage is the portrait of the glorified Jesus seated at the right hand of God in the previous verses. That will be an awesome thing to behold. There is power and majesty at the feet of Jesus that is so far above any power or majesty here on earth. A natural response to this power is fear. That's why so many times in the Bible stories, after people like Mary see an angel, their first response is fear. That's why Jesus says in Matthew 10:28, "Don't fear those who kill the body but are not able to kill the soul; rather, fear him who is able to destroy both soul and body in hell." We shouldn't fear cancer, for all it can do is kill the body. Instead, we should only fear God, whose judgment can result in the destruction of our souls as well as our bodies. There is an appropriate fear of someone with supreme glory and power.

But doesn't 2 Timothy 1:7 say that "God has not given us a spirit of fear, but one of power"? That is true. We were *not* given a spirit of fear, meaning we are not *rooted* in fear. We are rooted, by the Holy Spirit, in a spirit of power, love, and sound judgment. However, we still *feel* fear, obviously. We feel fear when we consider the awesome glory of God. We earnestly pray for faith, and for his faithfulness. We cry out for his mercy and grace day by day. We tremble at his power to save us, to heal us, for it is a *mighty* power. We fight the good fight of faith (1 Timothy 6:12) in "fear and trembling" because of the fact that it is a *fight*. If it weren't a fight, there'd be nothing to fear, nothing to tremble over. Our salvation is secure, but we still "work out our salvation" by fighting daily. Day by day we fight for faith against temptations that might lead us away from our God.

God's work is what enables you to do yours

We "work out our salvation with fear and trembling" because it is *God* who is working in us according to His good purposes. That's a fearful and wonderful thing!

God, the creator of the universe, is working in and through you!

Paul says we should tremble at such a thought. We should tremble that such powerful, wondrous, and awesome plans are being wrought in and through our lives. This truly is an amazingly fearful yet glorious thought to consider. Paul tells us that trembling at such a thought is a right and good response.

You can shine like stars in a dark world by holding firm to the word of life

What is God's "good purpose" for our cancer, that should cause us to tremble at the thought of it?

God's good purpose is that we shine like stars in a very dark world. His purpose is that unbelievers would see the hope we have in Christ Jesus and be saved. His purpose is that through our "holding firm" to his promises ("the *word* of life"), people would see that we are standing on a solid rock, fearless even in the face of death. Such faith is a very bright light that illuminates the entire room and is impossible for even unbelievers to ignore.

Pray for such faith! Pray that you would shine forth as a beacon, like a lighthouse, making people aware of the presence of Jesus in your life.

Prayer to the Lord

Heavenly Father, thank you for working in and through my life. You give my life meaning and purpose beyond anything this world can offer me. I tremble to know the God of the universe is at work personally in my life! Praise be to God! Grant me faith so that I would be a light for Christ in a dark world.

In Jesus' name, Amen.

Question to Consider

Is your conception of God devoid of any notion of fear or trembling? How might God be showing you a fuller, more complete, picture of himself?

Day 43

My Sacrifice Will Not Be for Nothing

Philippians 2:16b-18

Then I can boast in the day of Christ that I didn't run or labor for nothing. But even if I am poured out as a drink offering on the sacrificial service of your faith, I am glad and rejoice with all of you. In the same way you should also be glad and rejoice with me.

Here we see Paul boasting in the knowledge that his labor wasn't in vain, as well as rejoicing in his sacrifices that yield the fruit of faith and salvation for the Philippians.

What can we boast about in suffering?

The faith of the Philippians was Paul's reason for boasting. As we saw in verses 15-16a, he wanted to present the Philippians to the Lord as "blameless and pure, children of God who are faultless in a crooked and perverted generation, among whom you shine like stars in the world, by holding firm to the word of life." Like Paul, I want my family and others to be blameless and pure so that I can boast on the day of the Lord, knowing that I didn't suffer in vain.

Boasting means to make much of something. The word usually means something negative like pridefulness. However Paul uses the word here in a positive sense. It's good to make much of fruitful labor that results in the faith and salvation of others. Such work is the pinnacle of a purposeful, godly life.

Paul's boasting "in the day of Christ" reminds me of the parable of the talents (Matthew 25:14-30) where the master, before leaving on a journey, entrusted his servants with money to be used wisely while he was away. Of the three entrusted, two returned what they were given along with meaningful gains, while the third only returned what was given with no additional gains. In our lives, God has given to each of us talents and resources that we can use to bear fruit for the kingdom, or we can waste and squander the good things entrusted to us. The Lord will reward us for the fruit of our labor in heaven. Paul was eager to receive such rewards, and I am too.

As 1 Corinthians 3:13-14 says, "Each one's work will become manifest, for the Day will disclose it, because it will be revealed by fire, and the fire will test what sort of work each one has done. If the work that anyone has built on the foundation survives, he will receive a reward."

Why should we boast in our suffering?

Paul rejoiced in the sacrifices he made for the faith of the Philippians, first of all, because he loved them. It's not hard to want what is best for someone you love. In fact, many are even willing to die for their loved ones. Paul could boast in his suffering because he knew it was achieving salvation for those he loved. Secondly, Paul rejoiced in his suffering because of the rewards that will be given to him when he gets to heaven (1 Corinthians 3:13-14, 2 Timothy 4:8). Because of all this, Paul tells the Philippians, "Be glad and rejoice with me."

As friends and family offer their prayers for healing, encourage them to also offer their praise to God for the good work he's doing in you. Praise God for faith and fruitful labor, for your reward is great. Praise God for the testimony you now have after going through these deep waters. Even if you look back on your life and do not see much fruitful labor, rejoice even still. Even a simple faith in Jesus and a longing for Him to return yields heavenly reward, as we see in 2 Timothy 4:8:

> Now there is in store for me the crown of righteousness, which the Lord, the righteous Judge, will award to me on that day—and not only to me, but also to all who have longed for his appearing.

Prayer to the Lord

Lord, help me to live for you every day of my life. Help me to want your glory in your gospel even more than life itself, for your gospel is the power to save those who are lost. Use my cancer, oh Lord, so that the people around me would see the hope I have in Christ Jesus and be saved, and help me to find joy in your working through my circumstances.

In Jesus' name, Amen.

Question to Consider

Is there anyone in your life that you love even more than your life itself, such that it would be a joy to sacrifice everything for their faith and salvation? What is God calling you to do to be a blessing to them?

Day 44

Community as a Cure

Philippians 2:25-28

But I considered it necessary to send you Epaphroditus—my brother, coworker, and fellow soldier, as well as your messenger and minister to my need—since he has been longing for all of you and was distressed because you heard that he was sick. Indeed, he was so sick that he nearly died. However, God had mercy on him, and not only on him but also on me, so that I would not have sorrow upon sorrow. For this reason, I am very eager to send him so that you may rejoice again when you see him and I may be less anxious.

Often those who are well encourage those who are sick. I personally have been encouraged much by the company, prayers, and Bible verses sent to me by those who love me. Their love lessened my anxiety in my cancer considerably.

However, the sick can also be an encouragement to those who are well. In these verses we see Paul's eagerness to send Epaphroditus back to Philippi because the Philippians were anxious for him because they had heard he was deathly ill. Paul felt his presence with them would lessen their anxiety for him, especially since he had been healed. However, couldn't Paul have just told them he was healed and not to worry? Why did he need to send him? I think this is because their concern for Epaphroditus extended beyond the issue of his health.

Cancer can be very isolating. I often don't feel like hanging out with anybody. Engaging my wife and children takes considerable effort at times, especially when I am battling fear in addition to chemo/radiation symptoms. And yet, when I allow others into my fear, my pain, my anxiety, those are the times when I've been most encouraged. I've borrowed their faith, you might say.

There have also been times when others have borrowed mine. God had mercy on Epaphroditus and he recovered—we praise God that he was healed, and for all those who are healed. Testimonies of healing are powerful. However, God can also use sickness to bless and encourage those who are well, when they see our faith and hope in Jesus despite being unwell. I have personally been an encouragement to friends and family in this way, by God's grace.

The bottom line is that we see in these verses the importance of community, of the hands and feet of Jesus at work in the world to encourage the anxious. Don't give way to the isolating effects of cancer. To every degree possible, engage with others. Build them up even as they build you up. We are stronger together than we are alone. Pursue the fellowship of believers.

Prayer to the Lord

Lord Jesus, send people into my life to whom I can be a blessing, as well as being blessed by them. Help me not to walk this journey of cancer alone, but to be filled with the Spirit and be an encouragement to many, even as I desperately myself need encouragement.

In Jesus' name, Amen.

Question to Consider

Is there someone in your life who is deeply anxious about your cancer that you could encourage by showing them your hope in Christ? What are some ways you could do that?

Day 45

Treasure Beyond Comparison

Philippians 3

This chapter contains some of the most important verses in the Bible for cancer sufferers and their families. In it we learn of our hope for new bodies, perfect bodies at the resurrection, where our senses are perfectly tuned to fully experience our joy in the glory of God forever.

Because of this great hope for salvation, Paul says he considers all things as garbage by comparison. His goal is to know Christ, and all other worldly pursuits and pleasures just don't compare to knowing Jesus and attaining the promise of the resurrection.

This prize of new life gives us great hope in any affliction we encounter in our lifetimes. When you're diagnosed with cancer, you quickly realize how little you actually care about your possessions, wealth, and status. All of those things seem meaningless in that moment and give way to the solid rock of your hope in God and knowing Jesus, from which you are strengthened to battle cancer and fight for faith.

Take some time today to read this whole chapter and then we'll look closer at some key parts of it...

Philippians 3
Knowing Christ

In addition, my brothers and sisters, rejoice in the Lord. To write to you again about this is no trouble for me and is a safeguard for you.

2 Watch out for the dogs, watch out for the evil workers, watch out for those who mutilate the flesh. 3 For we are the circumcision, the ones who worship by the Spirit of God, boast in Christ Jesus, and do not put confidence in the flesh— 4 al-

though I have reasons for confidence in the flesh. If anyone else thinks he has grounds for confidence in the flesh, I have more: 5 circumcised the eighth day; of the nation of Israel, of the tribe of Benjamin, a Hebrew born of Hebrews; regarding the law, a Pharisee; 6 regarding zeal, persecuting the church; regarding the righteousness that is in the law, blameless.

7 But everything that was a gain to me, I have considered to be a loss because of Christ. 8 More than that, I also consider everything to be a loss in view of the surpassing value of knowing Christ Jesus my Lord. Because of him I have suffered the loss of all things and consider them as dung, so that I may gain Christ 9 and be found in him, not having a righteousness of my own from the law, but one that is through faith in Christ— the righteousness from God based on faith. 10 My goal is to know him and the power of his resurrection and the fellowship of his sufferings, being conformed to his death, 11 assuming that I will somehow reach the resurrection from among the dead.

Reaching Forward to God's Goal

12 Not that I have already reached the goal or am already perfect, but I make every effort to take hold of it because I also have been taken hold of by Christ Jesus. 13 Brothers and sisters, I do not consider myself to have taken hold of it. But one thing I do: Forgetting what is behind and reaching forward to what is ahead, 14 I pursue as my goal the prize promised by God's heavenly call in Christ Jesus. 15 Therefore, let all of us who are mature think this way. And if you think differently about anything, God will reveal this also to you. 16 In any case, we should live up to whatever truth we have attained. 17 Join in imitating me, brothers and sisters, and pay careful attention to those who live according to the example you have in us. 18 For I have often told you, and now say again with tears, that many live as enemies of the cross of Christ. 19 Their end is destruction; their god is their stomach; their glory is in their shame; and they are focused on earthly things. 20 Our citizenship is in heaven, and we eagerly wait for a Savior from there, the Lord Jesus Christ. 21 He will transform the body of our humble condition into the likeness of his glorious body, by the power that enables him to subject everything to himself.

Prayer to the Lord

Lord Jesus, thank you for revealing yourself to me. Help me to treasure your presence more than all other treasures on earth, for in you is my hope and salvation. Draw near to me, Lord.

In Jesus' name, Amen.

Question to Consider

What once held power over your affections but now seems as "dung"? Or, what still holds power over your affections, rivaling your affection for Jesus?

Day 46

No Confidence in the Flesh

Philippians 3:2-3

Watch out for the dogs, watch out for the evil workers, watch out for those who mutilate the flesh. For we are the circumcision, the ones who worship by the Spirit of God, boast in Christ Jesus, and do not put confidence in the flesh.

In these verses we see an important distinction that is key to surviving and even thriving through suffering...

The world puts their confidence in the flesh

The distinction in these verses all boils down to hoping in things that are seen vs. things that are unseen.

The specific context here is that Jewish Christians of the day believed in Jesus but also said everyone had to be circumcised in order to be saved. Their hope for salvation was still in "the flesh," i.e. their outward act of being circumcised.

However, Paul broadens the category of "evil workers" to anybody who puts their confidence in the flesh in any way. This reminds me of three things I used to trust in, and which, to some degree, I still do at my peril:

Most obvious to me was how *I trusted in my health* prior to my diagnosis. I was diagnosed with Esophageal Cancer at the age of 40 in the prime of my life. I was obsessive about getting stronger in the gym and I went jogging nearly every day. I was tracking my macros, watching my protein intake carefully, and consuming a full regimen of various supplements. My identity was in my health, and the irony is not lost on me at how vain those attempts were. At the height of my health, I was quite literally the most unhealthy I have ever been, and yet I had no idea. I thought I was on top of the world healthwise. Now it's clear that trusting in my attempts to be healthy is not a sure hope or a sure foundation to build my life upon.

The next temptation I faced was to *trust in my doctors too much*. I started treatment at arguably the best, most prestigious hospital in the world, the Mayo Clinic of Rochester, Minnesota. This isn't to say I don't think we shouldn't honor those doctors or trust their advice. This isn't to say we shouldn't pursue treatment with eagerness. Of course we should! But our contentment and joy should not be based on whether our doctors are right and their treatments make us better physically, because there's no guarantee that will happen. On the other hand, "we *know* that all things work together for the good" by God's providence (Romans 8:28) and that he will eventually heal us in heaven (Philippians 3:21).

We put our confidence in the Spirit

Another temptation is to *trust in being good*. We might think that God will heal us if we just do enough acts of kindness and avoid certain sins, or we might fall into the particular trap Paul is addressing in these verses. He's talking about how our confidence for salvation shouldn't be in good deeds we do (like being circumcised). Paul says this in Ephesians 2:8-9 also:

> For by grace you have been saved through faith. And this is not your own doing; it is the gift of God, not a result of works, so that no one may boast.

Believe in Jesus. That's it. That's where our ultimate confidence resides. *He* did the work for us on the cross, and we can trust him for it.

And this belief is fundamentally a confidence in things unseen, not things seen ("the flesh"). All throughout Philippians 3, Paul's confidence and strength amidst suffering is his hope in Christ Jesus. He knew that even if his body were to die, *he himself*, his spirit, would never die; he would live forever with Jesus. So his spirit worshiped God and boasted in Jesus.

Let us do likewise!

Prayer to the Lord

Lord God, thank you for opening my eyes to see your glory. Thank you for giving me spiritual eyes to see eternal things. I put my confidence in your Holy Spirit, Lord, not in the things seen here on earth. You, oh Lord, are the only true healer; through faith I am saved.

In Jesus' name, Amen.

Question to Consider

Has the Lord ever taken from you that which you had once been trusting in or idolizing? What did you learn from that experience?

Day 47

Everything is Rubbish Compared to Knowing Christ Jesus

Philippians 3:7-8

But everything that was a gain to me, I have considered to be a loss because of Christ. More than that, I also consider everything to be a loss in view of the surpassing value of knowing Christ Jesus my Lord. Because of him I have suffered the loss of all things and consider them as dung, so that I may gain Christ.

Wow! The bright and beautiful faith of Paul is such an inspiration. He saw with such clarity! Earlier in the book, he said that he would prefer to die and be with Christ (1:21-26), and here we see why. In his mind, no worldly pleasures could compare with knowing Christ Jesus. In fact, Paul considered the things of the world that he had gained as "dung" or rubbish compared with the surpassing value of his relationship with Jesus.

There are some obvious implications for cancer sufferers in this passage.

Everything that was gain no longer is

It's amazing how suffering, how cancer, brings into focus what is truly important in life. Never before have I had such depth of mental clarity into what is meaningful and what is rubbish. I've never been so purposeful with the time I have left. It really is too bad that it took cancer to bring this clarity, but the alternative is far worse.

I used to envy the cars people drove. Having five children,

we found it necessary to buy a large passenger van to haul them and their friends around town. I've always resented the need for it, desiring instead a car that would show off my social status and success. Now, however, that pursuit seems to me so vain, absurd even. It's the people *in* the car that I care about, not the car itself.

Another example was my idolizing of career advancement. For too long I found my identity in my success at work. Now, however, I'm very thankful that I don't have a team reporting to me; not only do I not need that added stress in my life right now, but I also see career advancement as "dung" when compared with the glory I see in the face of Jesus Christ.

The comparison to knowing Christ is the key

Paul compares the pleasures and blessings of this world to knowing Jesus and calls them "loss" and "dung." Cars and careers can be good things from God. However, when *compared* to knowing Jesus, they are rubbish.

This helps us to understand what Jesus had to say in Matthew 10:37-39:

> The one who loves a father or mother more than me is not worthy of me; the one who loves a son or daughter more than me is not worthy of me. And whoever doesn't take up his cross and follow me is not worthy of me. Anyone who finds his life will lose it, and anyone who loses his life because of me will find it.

Should we love our father and mother and honor them? Yes, of course. Should we love our children? Obviously. But even these, often the best blessings many receive in life, are incomparable to the glory and benefits of knowing and loving Christ Jesus. It's the comparison, the contrast, that Jesus is referring to, not that loving your parents and children is bad. It's this same comparison that Paul is making in Philippians 3.

Having cancer has given me this utter clarity. I love my wife and children more than anything else in this world. However, my relationship with Jesus is the only sure foundation that can hold me through this.

My wife and children cannot cure me of cancer. My wife and children cannot take away my fear of death. My wife and children cannot produce for me a hope of eternal life. Only Jesus can. And I love him immeasurably more because of the depths of this glorious hope I find in him.

Our desire is to gain Christ

I'm almost afraid to admit it, but being healed of cancer is also one of the "things" that fit in the "all things" bucket. It is very tempting to desire to be healed above all things, rather than to desire Jesus above all things.

I wrote the following paragraphs at a key time in my treatment:

> Yesterday I met with my doctor and he described the urgency to get started with Chemo. I'll admit it; the #1 thing on my mind was my desire to start chemo and be healed and my frustration at why it's taking so long to get started. In fact, for the two-hour car ride home, sullenness at this thought and desire for treatment was taking hold.
>
> It wasn't until I got home and re-read my way through the book of Philippians that I re-discovered what my true hope is, what I really desired above all things. In this short phrase, Paul describes why "all things," such as being cured of cancer, are "dung" compared to Jesus...because what he desired above all those things was attaining Jesus himself.
>
> And here's the deal: this is honestly a win/win. When I turn my face to Jesus, when I preach to myself his promises over me, I find that fear subsides and the sullenness is replaced with joy, and I'm thereby empowered to fight this cancer and to pursue healing! The often quoted verse, Philippians 4:13, "I can do all things through Christ Jesus who strengthens me," is no mere cliché! We are given the power to do "all things" when

we desire Jesus above all things.

I fight and have great hope for healing, but not because I want healing more than anything else. I have hope for healing because I believe in the power of the Healer to save and I want him more than anything else, even more than healing. Such affection for Jesus and the peace of God that flows from it is a miracle of God in the heart.

Prayer to the Lord

Lord Jesus, you are supremely valuable above and beyond all other things. Give me, Lord, more of your Holy Spirit. Draw near to me, oh my God, for you comfort me. I consider all things as dung compared to the awesome peace of God and the glory I see in Christ Jesus for me. I praise you, God, for I know I did not always have the eyes to see your supreme worth. Thank you for revealing your great worth to me so that I would see spiritual things more clearly.

In Jesus' name, Amen.

Question to Consider

Do you desire to be healed more than you desire Christ Jesus?

Day 48

Christ is My Righteousness

Philippians 3:8b-9

Because of [Christ] I have suffered the loss of all things and consider them as dung, so that I may gain Christ and be found in him, not having a righteousness of my own from the law, but one that is through faith in Christ—the righteousness from God based on faith.

Paul believed that the righteousness of Christ was the foundation of his salvation, not his good works. Isaiah 64:6 says our righteousness is like filthy rags compared to the holiness of God and the perfect standard set forth in his law. We cannot attain obedience to the full law of God. We aren't perfect, or even close to it.

But we know the One who was perfect. Jesus perfectly obeyed the law of God, which is why he was also the perfect sacrifice to cover the wrath of God for our sins. Paul says our righteousness comes through faith in this once-for-all sacrifice of Jesus. Thereby, Jesus' righteousness is given to us.

So we have great hope and confidence in our salvation and eternal life, not because we are "good" but because we believe in the one who really *was* good. Our confidence, our solid rock, our hope of eternal life, is in Jesus, not ourselves.

Is that true only for our confidence in eternal life, or for other things too, such as confidence in our battle with cancer? Later in Chapter 4 Paul will answer this for us when he says "I can do *all* things through [Christ] who strengthens me" (4:13). We'll dive deeper into that verse later, but suffice to say for now, the answer is *yes*. Jesus is our confidence and hope not only for the salvation of our souls when we die, but also for "all things," including our battle against cancer.

So many YouTubers and other influencers place their hope for healing in themselves, citing strategies such as "growth mindset" and eating a lot of broccoli and garlic. Mental models and dietary strategies can be helpful tools, but they are no solid rock on which to ground our confidence.

I have found that confidence in myself is shaky ground and a poor weapon against fear. My willpower is insufficient to see things in a positive light or to avoid thinking about my condition altogether. But when I turn to Jesus in prayer, reading his Word and praising His name, my feet touch a solid rock. Fear subsides and hope is renewed.

We weren't meant to fight this battle alone. And the only battle we're really meant to fight is the fight of faith, the fight to turn our eyes toward Jesus in the midst of stormy waters (see Matthew 14:22-33). So we don't put our trust in ourselves for our righteousness and salvation, nor do we put our trust in ourselves when we face hardship. Rather, we know that we can endure all things through Christ who strengthens us, and so we turn our eyes to Jesus when we suffer.

Our willpower won't get us through this, but Jesus can.

Prayer to the Lord

> *Lord God, be my strength in these dark waters, for my strength is not sufficient. I put my hope in you, oh Lord. You say you hold me by your righteous right hand; hold me, my God! Sustain me, I pray.*
>
> *In Jesus' name, Amen.*

Question to Consider

> *As you rank your trust in yourself, your doctors, and your God, which are you trusting in most at this moment?*

Day 49

My Goal

Philippians 3:10-11

My goal is to know him and the power of his resurrection and the fellowship of his sufferings, being conformed to his death, assuming that I will somehow reach the resurrection from among the dead.

Paul's main objective in life was to know Christ Jesus better and to live in that knowledge. We see four facets of that knowledge in these verses, and how they cause him to live in a newness of life that we too can take courage from.

Know Christ and the power of His resurrection

Paul wants to know Jesus' power over death, and it's obvious why. For the past few chapters Paul has been describing his assumed imminent death, but he's also been describing for us his confidence in death, i.e. "to live is Christ, to die is gain." Where does such confidence come from? It comes from knowing the power of Christ Jesus over death; it comes from knowing Jesus defeated death and is Lord over it.

I'm reminded of the story of the resurrection of Lazarus in John 11:38-44. Jesus asked for the stone of Lazarus' tomb to be removed but Martha resisted, saying that since he had been dead for four days, there would be a bad smell. Jesus replied, "Didn't I tell you that if you believed you would see the glory of God?" Jesus prayed to God that the bystanders would believe in him as a result of what he was about to do, and then he commanded Lazarus to come out of the tomb. The dead man was resurrected, and many of the Jews came to believe in Jesus as a result of this miracle.

What's even more amazing is that Jesus raised himself from the dead! We have the evidence of 500+ witnesses for that greatest-of-all miracles. In that and the raising of Lazarus, we see Jesus' absolute power over death. And knowing this brings us great hope. It brought Paul immense confidence in the face of death, and it can bring us that confidence as well. We know that even if we die, we will *never* die. We know our spirit will never die. Though we will die physically if Christ doesn't return first, within one millisecond our souls will be taken up to be with him forever. That is the power of his resurrection for us.

Know Christ and the fellowship of his sufferings

Paul wanted to know "the fellowship of [Christ's] sufferings." I believe this means he wanted to be in communion with Jesus' sufferings, to suffer as Christ suffered, but also to be in the community of believers who likewise suffered.

For what reason did Jesus suffer? He suffered to do the will of God, and he suffered because the world hated him because he was the light of the world and the world preferred darkness (John 3:19).

In John 15:18-21 Jesus tells us that all who are in Him will suffer in a similar way:

> If the world hates you, understand that it hated me be-fore it hated you. If you were of the world, the world would love you as its own. However, because you are not of the world, but I have chosen you out of it, the world hates you. Remember the word I spoke to you: "A servant is not greater than his master." If they persecuted me, they will also perse-cute you. If they kept my word, they will also keep yours. But they will do all these things to you on ac-count of my name because they don't know the one who sent me.

Paul wanted to be in this community of sufferers, because "the sufferings of this present time are not worth comparing with the glory that is going to be revealed to us" (Romans 8:18). A little suffering now will give way to an eternal weight of glory that makes our suffering today seem "light" and "momentary" (2 Corinthians 4:17-18).

Know Christ and be conformed to His death

How did Jesus die? He died doing the will of his Father. What is the will of God? Jesus says the entire law of God, his will for us, is summed up in two commands: 1) to love God, and 2) to love others (Matthew 22:37-40). Jesus demonstrates ultimate obedience to the will of God by dying for us on the cross—he shows that he loves God even more than life, and he shows that he loves *us* even more than life.

Paul wants to be conformed to this death, a death marked by an extreme love for God and an extreme love for people to the point that he's willing to die for those he loves.

This is a great example for me as a cancer sufferer. I've often said, off hand, that I'd be willing to take a bullet for my wife or kids. But what if God is going to use my cancer, even my death perhaps, to turn their eyes away from themselves and instead to Jesus, for their salvation? Is that something I'd be willing to die for? Of course. Similarly, Paul was willing to be imprisoned and executed for the sake of spreading the gospel in the Roman empire, because of his love for those who were being saved.

If we die from cancer, but we die in a similar way to Christ Jesus' death, our death is not in vain. Our death will be marked by love, love for God and love for those around us, and God may use that love in a thousand ways we will never know until we come to be with Him in heaven.

Know Christ and assume you too will be resurrected from the dead

Paul says that he "assumes" that he will "somehow" reach the resurrection from the dead. Paul doesn't use the word "assume" and "somehow" to suggest he's operating on blind faith; he *knows* he'll be raised from the dead, and he knows how he'll be raised (Christ's power). And yet he uses these words of ambiguity to show us that there's still mystery in this resurrection, there's still faith in something unseen. He knows it to be true, but that doesn't make the power of God any less unfathomable, unsearchable, to our little brains.

I think we can take courage from this. Paul's faith often seems impeccable, like he's some kind of "super Christian." To a degree he is—he literally heard the voice of Jesus on the Damascus Road, was called as an Apostle, and was "caught up to the third heaven" (2 Corinthians 12:2). But in this passage we see he still is a mere human with uncertainties. He could not fully comprehend the mind of God and how exactly Jesus will raise him from the dead. And yet he "assumes" he will be resurrected, and "somehow" it'll happen. We too can be assured and confident in our resurrection while still leaving room for mystery and faith.

Prayer to the Lord

> *Father God, help me to be more like your Son Jesus, to seek first your kingdom and to sacrificially love those you've put in my life, and even to love my enemies as Jesus did. I know a life lived full of love is a life not wasted. And so, just as Jesus lived and died for the love of others, help me to do the same.*

> *In Jesus' name, Amen.*

Question to Consider

> *How should an expectation of resurrection transform how you live?*

Day 50

Pursuing the Prize

Philippians 3:12-14

Not that I have already reached the goal or am already perfect, but I make every effort to take hold of [the resurrection] because I also have been taken hold of by Christ Jesus. Brothers and sisters, I do not consider myself to have taken hold of it. But one thing I do: Forgetting what is behind and reaching forward to what is ahead, I pursue as my goal the prize promised by God's heavenly call in Christ Jesus.

There are so many beautiful words of encouragement for us in these few verses. I count four key ideas, but you may see more.

Paul wasn't perfect

It's easy to put Paul on a pedestal. It's easy to put Christian leaders in general on pedestals. We tend to only see the best sides of them. Too often we assume they are the model, perfect Christians.

In Paul we see a man filled with faith, eager to lay down his life for the sake of the gospel. He is constantly encouraging the believers and modeling for them how to live a life of faith. He seems the perfect Christian. But he's not. Only Jesus was.

For me, Paul's words are a reminder that my ups and downs are normal. It's normal for my faith to ebb and flow. It's a fight for faith; I'm not yet perfect, either.

Cancer in particular is a heavy burden. I hope nobody puts me on a pedestal just because I wrote a book. Anybody can write a book; it doesn't really mean anything, honestly. A lot of wolves in sheep's clothing write books to make themselves look good.

No, I am not perfect, and neither are you. Tears of fear and doubt all too often plague me. But thanks be to God that Jesus has taken hold of me, and he carries me through those ebbs and back into the flowing grace of his presence and peace.

Jesus has taken hold of us

Paul fights on because Jesus has taken hold of him. I feel the same way.

Even in the depths of my despair, my hope in Christ Jesus somehow always remains. It seems that the Lord has taken hold of me by His righteous right hand, as he says in Isaiah 41:10: "So do not fear, for I am with you; do not be dismayed, for I am your God. I will strengthen you and help you; I will uphold you with my righteous right hand."

For those of us who are in Christ, we are *held*, and he is faithful to hold us through our darkest troubles. Nothing truly bad can happen to us, because even if we die, God will continue to hold us and carry us through death into eternal life. We are *held*, my friends. Believe that, and you will be strengthened to endure anything.

Therefore we pursue as our goal the promised prize

Since we are "held," we can pursue the goal of resurrection and eternal life.

It's easy to believe in "the afterlife." Billions have done so. Billions have said "they are in a better place" when friends or family die. But we in Christ Jesus have a sure confidence in that statement that most do not have.

We are held by God, and therefore can pursue our prize of resurrected bodies in confidence that we will *indeed* get them. Our trust is in Jesus, not ourselves. Jesus is holding us, and will carry us from death to life. We pursue our goal knowing we *will* receive it.

What place does fear have in our lives when we believe something so astounding? Praise be to God for faith in Christ

Jesus to carry us through the storm and to our prize of eternal life!

Forget the past, reach for what is ahead

For all the aforementioned reasons, we can forget the past and live in eager expectation for the future.

For me, this meant moving beyond trying to understand how I gave myself cancer. I'd been hyper-analyzing all my behaviors and habits and trying to figure out which one of them caused my condition. What made this distressing was that, by and large, I'd actually been living a rather robust and healthy life. I was only 40 years old; I ate well and exercised 5-6 days per week. What could it be?

But such obsessing was futile. I did not give myself cancer.

We all are at risk for all kinds of calamity simply because we live in a fallen, sinful world.

God is using your cancer for your good, for the spread of the hope you have in Christ, and for the glory of his name. You can forget the past, knowing God is for you, not against you; he has you held by his righteous right hand and you can look forward to the future.

Prayer to the Lord

> *Lord God, thank you for giving me life this day. Thank you for creating me and sustaining me until this moment. Help me, this day, to live for you. Your command to me is to love well; help me to do that today and every day you give me.*
>
> *In Jesus' name, Amen.*

Question to Consider

> *What is something from your past you need to put aside and move on from mentally and emotionally?*

Day 51

Live Up to the Truth You Have Attained

Philippians 3:15-17

Therefore, let all of us who are mature think this way. And if you think differently about anything, God will reveal this also to you. In any case, we should live up to whatever truth we have attained. Join in imitating me, brothers and sisters, and pay careful attention to those who live according to the example you have in us.

Paul has two commands for us in these verses, both of which are important to obey in the midst of our suffering.

Live up to whatever truth you have attained

I've had the good fortune to get connected with some cancer patients who have been through the same diagnosis and treatment that I'm going through. It was very encouraging to hear their stories, since they were so similar to my own. They brought me great hope for curative treatment; they beat the odds, and maybe I will too.

One refrain that I kept hearing from them was how their faith in Jesus crystallized in the first weeks after their diagnosis; they had to depend on him wholly. They read their Bibles and prayed constantly, in a few cases for the first time in their lives. In the midst of overwhelming fear, where else could we go for comfort and peace? Nothing compares.

However, a few of them confided in me that as they got settled into their treatment plans and scans started coming back clean, it was easy to settle into old ways of false confidence in their flesh. They were tempted to rely on themselves and not on God when times were good, and the disciplines of seeking the Lord in prayer and Scripture slipped away.

A key blessing that comes from cancer is that we learn to rely on God and not ourselves. We learn that God is real, he loves us, and he's reliable. We should strive to live up to this truth all our days, in the good times and the bad. It's a hard-won truth that I hope I never need to relearn.

Imitate Paul and others who live for Christ

Paul tells us that we should strive to become more like him and others who are following his example. All throughout the book of Philippians we've seen his sacrificial faith and love for others, considering others as more important than himself. Paul's own role model, Jesus, demonstrated this selfless love in the most ultimate way, and he also commanded us to follow his example.

Those we surround ourselves with tend to be the kind of people we become. So give consideration to those you spend time with; are you becoming more like them or are they becoming more like you? Find people you can imitate who will point you continually to Jesus, and be the type of person who continually points others toward Jesus. This is Paul's example to us.

Prayer to the Lord

> *Father God, thank you for revealing yourself to me in Christ Jesus. Thank you for opening my eyes to see your glory and opening my ears to perceive your truth and promises for me. By your power, oh Lord, I pray help me to walk in this spirit of truth and never again walk in a spirit of darkness. Help me never to take for granted Christ's death on the cross. Take my life, oh Lord, refine it and use it for your kingdom, I pray.*
>
> *In Jesus' name, Amen.*

Question to Consider

Are there any brothers or sisters in your life whose faith you strive to imitate, who build you up in the faith with every interaction? How can you pursue community with them more frequently? And who in your life tends to tear you down or draw you away from faith in Christ? What steps should you take to distance yourself from that individual?

Day 52

Hope for New Bodies

Philippians 3:20-4:1

Our citizenship is in heaven, and we eagerly wait for a Savior from there, the Lord Jesus Christ. He will transform the body of our humble condition into the likeness of his glorious body, by the power that enables him to subject everything to himself. So then, my dearly loved and longed for brothers and sisters, my joy and crown, in this manner stand firm in the Lord, dear friends.

These verses are some of the most encouraging verses in the entire Bible for cancer sufferers. We are encouraged to look forward to our true home and citizenship in heaven, where we'll receive our glorified, perfect bodies.

Our citizenship is in heaven, not on earth

When faced with cancer, the thought of leaving this earth just seems scary. It's not what we want. We want to stay, to remain here. It feels like our citizenship is on earth, like we belong here. But the truth is we belong with Jesus—our true citizenship is in heaven with him.

Even when we are healthy, there's a part of our spirit that groans to be with Jesus; we feel incomplete here on earth. This feeling testifies that our true citizenship is in heaven. Paul says we "eagerly wait for a Savior from there." We shouldn't suppress that yearning to be with Jesus face to face, in person. It's a good thing!

It's also natural and good to want to live, for Paul says earlier in this letter that he did want to "remain" for the progress and joy of his loved ones' faith. So, it's good to eagerly want to be with the Lord, and it's good to want to live, assuming the desire to live is rooted in serving the Lord and being a blessing to others. But we need to remember where we truly belong. We belong with Jesus, and only then will our joy be made full.

We should want our joy to be full. Our joy has never been full here on earth; it has always been only a partial joy even at the best of times. When we enter into paradise, however, our joy will be full because we will be where we are meant to be—forever.

We will get new, glorious bodies

The book of Genesis tells us that the Lord God spoke and everything that exists was created by the power of his word. This power of God is astonishing, and this power is our hope for resurrection and new bodies.

In this passage in Philippians, Paul tells us plainly that our bodies will be transformed from these broken, cancer-ridden bodies into glorious bodies perfectly crafted for our senses to experience the glory of God in the fullest possible extent. New eyes. New ears. New taste buds. New senses of touch. All our senses will be gloriously attuned to experience the glory of God, to worship him forever, and to feel the fullness of joy forever.

We won't be spirits floating around aimlessly in the clouds. We will be given bodies, akin to the bodies we have now, but perfected. No cancer. No pain. All of our senses heightened to their maximum capacity for joy.

Therefore, we can stand firm

This astonishing hope in Christ Jesus and his power is a solid rock on which we can stand. This hope is an antidote to fear. Death only ushers in our glory. Death brings us home. And knowing this hope, believing in this expectation of salvation, enables us to live today to the fullest extent possible.

We can live today and be a blessing to others, with every

breath we're given, because we have in us a spirit of power and love, and *not* a spirit of fear (2 Timothy 1:7). Our hope in Christ Jesus pushes down fear and this spirit of power wells up within us to replace it, enabling us to live for Christ and to love those whom God has put in our lives.

This is what "standing firm" looks like, friends. It looks like taking up the power of Jesus for us and loving well those we encounter.

It means showing them the hope you have in Christ Jesus even in the midst of cancer.

It means being a blessing, and not being a slave to fear.

I say all this as if preaching to myself. I want you to know that it isn't easy for me, either. Faith is a fight. We fight the good fight of faith (1 Timothy 6:12). I pray for this faith, this power, this hope, to fill me. I pray this every day, because if I don't, I start feeling the fear rise up.

Don't put me on a pedestal here, folks. Feel free to put Jesus on a pedestal, but even Jesus in the garden of Gethsemane had fear; his sweat was like drops of blood (Luke 22:44). Jesus felt intense fear, but he got down on his knees and prayed to God for strength, and God strengthened him (Luke 22:43). Let us do likewise, without ceasing.

Pray until you feel your feet touch that solid rock.

Prayer to the Lord

> *Lord Jesus, thank you for preparing a place for me in heaven! Thank you for the hope I have in the promise of a new body at the resurrection! I know that even if I die, I will never die. I will be with you forever. Thank you Jesus. Help me to stand firm in this hope, not fearing anything.*
>
> *In Jesus' name, Amen.*

Question to Consider

> *How does the knowledge of our promise for new physical bodies, rather than the typical vague*

sentiments of our spirits "going to heaven," shape your hope for eternity and impact how you live today?

Day 53

Contentment and Cancer

Philippians 4

Paul concludes his letter to the Philippians by encouraging them to set their minds on things that are praiseworthy, honorable, and true. This requires an intentional, dedicated act of setting our focus on eternal truths and not giving way to fear or doubts.

In fact, later in the chapter Paul tells us that he has learned to be content in all circumstances. This includes contentment in poverty or plenty, as well as in sickness or in health. Such contentment, along with setting his mind on that which is praiseworthy, is possible because he can do all things through Christ who strengthens him.

We too can be content, even amidst cancer, because Jesus is a rich fountain of strength and hope.

Before we look at some important parts of the chapter, take some time today to read all of it...

Philippians 4

"So then, my dearly loved and longed for brothers and sisters, my joy and crown, in this manner stand firm in the Lord, dear friends.
Practical Counsel
2 I urge Euodia and I urge Syntyche to agree in the Lord. 3 Yes, I also ask you, true partner, to help these women who have contended for the gospel at my side, along with Clement and the rest of my coworkers whose names are in the book of life. 4 Rejoice in the Lord always. I will say it again: Rejoice! 5 Let your graciousness be known to everyone. The Lord is near. 6 Don't worry about anything, but in everything, through prayer and petition with thanksgiving, present your requests to God. 7 And

the peace of God, which surpasses all understanding, will guard your hearts and minds in Christ Jesus.

8 Finally brothers and sisters, whatever is true, whatever is honorable, whatever is just, whatever is pure, whatever is lovely, whatever is commendable—if there is any moral excellence and if there is anything praiseworthy—dwell on these things. 9 Do what you have learned and received and heard from me, and seen in me, and the God of peace will be with you.

Appreciation of Support

10 I rejoiced in the Lord greatly because once again you renewed your care for me. you were, in fact, concerned about me but lacked the opportunity to show it. 11 I don't say this out of need, for I have learned to be content in whatever circumstances I find myself. 12 I know how to make do with little, and I know how to make do with a lot. In any and all circumstances I have learned the secret of being content— whether well fed or hungry, whether in abundance or in need. 13 I am able to do all things through him who strengthens me. 14 Still, you did well by partnering with me in my hardship.

15 And you Philippians know that in the early days of the gospel, when I left Macedonia, no church shared with me in the matter of giving and receiving except you alone. 16 For even in Thessalonica you sent gifts for my need several times. 17 Not that I seek the gift, but I seek the profit that is increasing to your account. 18 But I have received everything in full, and I have an abundance. I am fully supplied, having received from Epaphroditus what you provided—a fragrant offering, an acceptable sacrifice, pleasing to God. 19 And my God will supply all your needs according to his riches in glory in Christ Jesus. 20 Now to our God and Father be glory forever and ever. Amen.

Final Greetings

21 Greet every saint in Christ Jesus. The brothers who are with me send you greetings. 22 All the saints send you greetings, especially those who belong to Caesar's household. 23 The grace of the Lord Jesus Christ be with your spirit."

Prayer to the Lord

Lord God, thank you for your peace. Help me to trust you in all circumstances, oh Lord. Lead me by still waters and comfort my soul. Your glory, oh Lord, is my hope and strength.

In Jesus' name, Amen.

Question to Consider

In what ways has your contentment grown since entering the fiery trial of cancer?

Day 54

Rejoice Always

Philippians 4:4

Rejoice in the Lord always.
I will say it again: Rejoice!

It's important that we remember the goodness of God even in the most difficult times. In this verse Paul tells us to rejoice in the Lord *always*. Always is the key word, and rejoicing always requires a miracle of the Holy Spirit in our hearts, because at times it's the last thing we would naturally be inclined to do.

Rejoicing means finding joy in something and celebrating the good that God will bring from that thing. We can rejoice in the Lord amidst cancer because we know where our hope comes from; our hope comes from the Lord. Hope for salvation. Hope for healing. Hope for comfort and the pushing down of fear. Hope for a meaningful life. Hope for new bodies.

Such an astonishing hope is cause for joy and celebration, because it points to a weight of glory so far beyond comparison to these present sufferings (2 Corinthians 4:17). Since our hope is in the Lord, we can rejoice in the Lord at all times.

Never stop rejoicing in the Lord.

When you feel anger at the Lord for getting cancer, express that anger to him in prayer like David did in the Psalms (see Psalm 13:1-2). But don't forget to also rejoice in the truths he has for you; truths you cling to even in the midst of anger (see Psalm 13:2-6). And do that for all other emotions that get in the way of your rejoicing. Convey those emotions to the Lord in prayer, and then rejoice for the things the Lord has done for you that have given you hope.

Rejoice ceaselessly.

Prayer to the Lord

Lord God, you are so good to me. Thank you Jesus for the hope I have in you, for you have saved me and are saving me day by day. I rejoice in knowing you, Jesus, for when all other hopes fall apart, you, oh Lord, are never shaken—you remain my solid rock and strength through the storm. Praise hallelujah! I praise your great name! Help me, oh Lord, to praise your name even in the midst of fear and doubt; help me not to forget all you've done for me nor will do for me in the future.

In Jesus' name, Amen.

Question to Consider

Is there someone you know who has always rejoiced in the Lord even during suffering? What do you recall of their faith and experience? Are they available to get together for some mutual encouragement? If not, consider reading the book The Heavenly Man, *a story of a Chinese Christian who was severely persecuted for his faith and yet remained faithful.*

Day 55

The Lord's Presence and Peace

Philippians 5:5b-7

The Lord is near. Don't worry about anything, but in everything, through prayer and petition with thanksgiving, present your requests to God. And the peace of God, which surpasses all understanding, will guard your hearts and minds in Christ Jesus.

Here Paul says that we don't have to worry about anything because the Lord is near to us, and that when we pray we should always do so with thanksgiving. That kind of prayer would be impossible if not for the peace of God, which guards our hearts and minds.

The Lord is near and you don't have to worry

A temptation to be worried or anxious always seems to be on the doorstep in a battle with cancer, and that can lead to many other spiritual and emotional problems, as well as possibly delaying our healing. However, we're told we don't have to worry. Why?

Because the Lord is near.

God is with us, friends. When you start to worry, go to him! Go to him in prayer. Go to his words by reading your Bible. Go to him in praise and thanksgiving through worship music. Go to him and you will find that he is near, and his peace will replace worry and other harmful invaders of your heart.

Make your requests to God with thanksgiving

Here Paul tells us that we should pray with thankfulness "in everything," and "everything" includes our prayers about cancer. How do we pray for healing with thanksgiving?

I think the most obvious answer is that we know we *will* be healed—either in this life or the next. Unbelievers do not have this astonishing hope; they are not confident in their salvation and their new, perfected, resurrected bodies. However, we who are in Christ Jesus can be.

We know that "to die is gain" (Philippians 1:21) and we "long to be with Christ, which would be far better" (Philippians 1:23). We trust that our broken, humble bodies will be transformed into glorious, perfect bodies (Philippians 3:20-4:1). And yet we plead earnestly for healing of our earthly bodies, which is right and good to do. However, unlike the unbeliever, we also give our thankful praise for our certain *expectation* of glorious, perfect bodies.

We can also pray for healing from cancer with thanksgiving because we know that God is working this cancer for our good, as Paul says in Romans: "We know that in all things God works for the good of those who love him, who have been called according to his purpose" (Romans 8:28).

That verse is often viewed as a cliché, but it is a powerful promise nonetheless. For some reason I always cringe when people quote this verse to me, and yet its truth is undeniable. God has done amazing things in my life for me and those around me through my cancer. I went from a functional atheist to wholly trusting in Jesus, praying ceaselessly, and believing in Him fervently—all within a few hours of receiving my diagnosis. Praise be to God! I thank God! I pray for healing, but I would never want to go back to my former self, who was so ignorant and taking everything for granted.

The peace of God will guard your heart and mind

The peace of God guards our *hearts* from worry, fear, etc. by bringing to remembrance the truths and promises of God that we can use to fight against such temptations—truths like his nearness, his holding us by his righteous right hand, and his power to heal.

The peace of God will also guard our *minds* by reminding us that we are not a statistic, that the battle belongs to the Lord, and that while we'll honor our doctors and treatment plans, we will not trust in them. We'll trust in the Lord. The peace of God will also deliver to us confidence in our salvation and eternal life, so that when thoughts of death arise, we will see how it can only serve to make us stronger.

Normal people don't feel or think this way. Normal people's hearts and minds don't behave like this. The peace of God surpasses understanding; it is a miracle of the Holy Spirit in our lives.

Seek the peace of God with all fervor and zeal! The Lord is near, but faith is still a fight against the enemy. Pray. Praise. And pursue his word for you in the Holy Bible. God is gracious in giving out his peace when we seek him.

Knock, my friends, and the door will be opened unto you (Matthew 7:7-8).

Prayer to the Lord

> *Father God, draw near to me. Holy Spirit, comfort me in my distress. Thank you Jesus for revealing yourself, for opening my eyes to see your glory and to believe your promises for me. Lord, please hear my cries for mercy! In the power of Jesus' name, heal my body, oh God I pray. Thank you for the confidence I have in knowing that indeed one day I will be healed. Guard my heart and my mind from fear and worry. Set my hope on Christ Jesus, this day and every day.*
>
> *In Jesus' name, Amen.*

Question to Consider

> *When in your life have you felt most "near" to the Lord, and what were the circumstances surrounding that?*

Day 56

Dwell on What is Honorable

Philippians 4:8-9

Finally brothers and sisters, whatever is true, whatever is honorable, whatever is just, whatever is pure, whatever is lovely, whatever is commendable—if there is any moral excellence and if there is anything praiseworthy—dwell on these things. Do what you have learned and received and heard from me, and seen in me, and the God of peace will be with you.

In my cancer journey I've found that if I try to suppress my feelings or run away from my emotions, things only get worse.

For example, my natural inclination is to escape from my feelings into binging on video games. I'm not saying playing a video game is bad, *per se*, but rather my motivation to do so often is. The result is always that I feel worse afterwards, because by seeking escape I am not actually dealing with my feelings, but just trying to avoid them. When I do come up for air, I usually feel worse than when I started.

On the other hand, when I keep my eyes on Jesus I am continually built up. As an alternative to video games, I've been listening to audio books about theology. If I'm feeling depressed, I go on a walk and listen to the Word of God being explained and taught. By the time I come home, the fear and sadness has often left me and I'm ready to jump back into my day with new vigor.

What builds you up may be different from what builds me up. Likewise, some things that tear you down may actually be an encouragement to someone else. However, Philippians 4:8 tells us that these are always good to dwell on: things that are true, honorable, just, pure, lovely, commendable, morally excellent, and praiseworthy.

Our spiritual life is described in the Scriptures as a battle (Ephesians 6:10-17, 2 Timothy 4:7). Fighting is the opposite of escaping or running away. Fighting means turning toward the feelings and emotions and warring against the world, the flesh, and the devil by setting our minds on what is true and praiseworthy. Then our enemies will be defeated.

Hour by hour I must do this, because if I don't, depression quickly takes a foothold in my heart. On the other hand, when I turn to Jesus, sadness is cast out.

I pray that you, too, would turn to what is true and praiseworthy. Flee from what tears you down. Run toward Jesus.

Prayer to the Lord

> *Lord Jesus, you are true, honorable, just, pure, lovely, commendable, morally excellent, and praiseworthy. Help me to continually turn to you for encouragement. Help me not to seek worldly escapes from my feelings and emotions, but rather to turn toward what is true so that your promises for me would take hold, not my fear or sadness. For I've been given this spirit of power, love, and sound judgment, and I've not been given a spirit of fear. Thank you, Lord, for giving me this power to fight for faith, to fight against fear and sadness.*
>
> *In Jesus' name, Amen.*

Question to Consider

> *When I was diagnosed, I "fasted" from video games for several months. What might the Lord be calling you to fast from and instead turn to Him for comfort?*

Day 57

Content in All Circumstances

Philippians 4:11b-12

*I have learned to be content in whatever circum-
stances I find myself. I know how to make do with
little, and I know how to make do with a lot. In
any and all circumstances I have learned the
secret of being content—whether well fed or
hungry, whether in abundance or in need.*

Paul says he has learned to be content in whatever circumstances he finds himself in. I think we need to define the word
"content" just to show how absolutely mind-blowing this statement is, considering all the hardship, persecution, and health
issues Paul had to endure.

What is contentment? Contentment is feeling or showing
satisfaction with one's possessions, status, or situation. Defining the opposite may be helpful as well. Discontentedness is
the condition of being dissatisfied with one's life or situation.

It is startling to hear of Paul's satisfaction in all his circumstances. We know he was severely persecuted (Acts 20:23). We
know he had to work hard to provide for himself; he was not
wealthy (Acts 18:3). We know he had health issues (2 Corinthians 12). We know he was imprisoned multiple times (Philippians 1:12-14). We know he was severely beaten on several
occasions, even near to the point of death (2 Corinthians 1:9).

How could he be content through all that suffering? The
explanation of his "thorn in the flesh" in 2 Corinthians 12:7-10
sheds some light on this question:

Therefore, so that I would not exalt myself, a
thorn in the flesh was given to me, a messenger

of Satan to torment me so that I would not exalt myself. Concerning this, I pleaded with the Lord three times that it would leave me. But he said to me, "My grace is sufficient for you, for my power is perfected in weakness." Therefore, I will most gladly boast all the more about my weaknesses, so that Christ's power may reside in me. So I take pleasure in weaknesses, insults, hardships, persecutions, and in difficulties, for the sake of Christ. For when I am weak, then I am strong.

Think about the following observations from that passage:

God allowed his health issue so that he would not exalt himself

Apparently Paul had some kind of humiliating health issue. We never learn exactly what his issue was, but we can see that it kept him from being prideful. Some have speculated that it could have been a speech impediment or a grotesque eye malady. Regardless of what it was, however, we know that Paul believed his problem was being used by God for good purposes in his life and the lives of others.

He pleaded with the Lord to be healed but wasn't

It is reassuring to know that Paul desperately wanted to be healed. We can be content *and* want to be healed at the same time. Contentment in cancer doesn't mean the absence of a desire for healing. It means we can desperately want to be healed, but yet we are satisfied in God no matter the outcome.

God's grace was sufficient for Paul—and us—and God's power is seen best in our weaknesses

God chose not to heal Paul in this life, saying that the grace he had given to Paul was enough and healing wasn't necessary for Paul's ministry.

Interestingly, God said His grace is sufficient because his

power is perfected in weakness. This is the opposite of what we'd assume, which is that God's power looks more glorious in a healing than someone not being healed. However, Paul's contentment in not being healed makes the glory of the power of God look even more glorious than if God had healed him, because Paul's contentment itself is an amazing demonstration of God's power in his life.

Whether we are healed of cancer or not, God's power is on display in our lives when we display contentment in God.

Paul takes pleasure in hardships "for the sake of Christ"

Paul takes pleasure in hardships like his health issue because they are opportunities to make much of Christ. God's glory is revealed to himself and others through his faith and perseverance in trials. So Paul rejoices in suffering because his chief priority is to make much of Christ and bring glory to God, not to be healed.

So, back to Philippians 4:11-12, how was Paul able to be content in all circumstances? What is the "secret of being content?" We see the answer in verse 13: "I am able to do all things through him who strengthens me."

Paul was able to be content in all circumstances because Christ Jesus gave him strength to be content, and Jesus gives strength in abundance to those who desire the glory of Christ Jesus to be on display.

Finally, we shouldn't miss the word "learned" used by Paul in verse 12. Paul *learned* to be content. Through the repeated necessity of relying on Jesus, he learned that Jesus can hold him through any trial. You could say, then, that relying on God is just as much a skill as it is an act. The more you rely on him, the better you become at relying on him. This learning happens when we see the power of God in our past and therefore trust in God for our future.

So here's the biblical formula for contentment: 1) bring to remembrance how God has shown up for you in your past, 2) have faith that God will likewise show up for you in your future, 3) desire the glory of Jesus to be magnified in your life above any desires for your circumstances, and 4) trust that Christ will supply you with the strength you need to bring glory to his name through your contentment.

Prayer to the Lord

Lord God, help me to be content in all circumstances. Help me to desire your glory in my life more than all other desires. Such contentment and desire for your glory are not natural to me; work in me your Holy Spirit to give me these desires. Strengthen me, Christ Jesus, to trust in you as I walk with cancer. Only you can do this work in my heart, oh Lord. Do it, I pray, and be glorified through me.

In Jesus' name, Amen.

Question to Consider

What do you desire more than God being glorified in your life? Confess that sin to God and ask him to change your heart by the power of the Spirit.

Day 58

Get and Give Help

Philippians 4:14

You did well by partnering with me in my hardship.

We discussed on Day 57 how Paul learned to be content in all circumstances through Christ Jesus who gave him strength to be content. I don't mean to rehash all that here except to add verse 14 onto the end of Paul's treatise on contentment. In the previous passage Paul says that he has learned to be content in whatever circumstances because he is strengthened by Christ to do so. Then in verse 14 he adds that the Philippians did well to partner with him in his hardship, which means that Paul didn't endure the hardship alone. He had help.

Especially for those of us who live in the U.S., it can be easy to assume that Paul's contentment resulted from his own self-determination and individualistic willpower. But this is clearly not the case. Paul's courage in the face of hardship was empowered through Christ Jesus' power working in Paul. It was Christ who gave Paul the strength he needed to be content in his circumstances.

And in verse 14 we also see that in addition to Christ's work inside Paul, a host of people gathered around Paul to support him during his hardship (which was still Christ at work, of course, just in a different way).

So the bottom line is that you shouldn't fight cancer alone. Don't try to walk through these deep waters by yourself. Contentment in cancer is not an individual achievement; it is a community endeavor.

In the first weeks after my diagnosis, I reached out to everybody I could think of and daily lined up someone to talk with. I needed the body of believers around me like never before in my life. My wife certainly was a critical support, and still is, but she too was a broken vessel. Collectively we needed others to support us, and still do. Sometimes life deals a burden too heavy for two people to carry, let alone one.

And if Paul wasn't such a "super Christian" that he didn't need the help of others, you too need the body of Christ around you to help partner in your hardship. And like Paul, the best way to get the help of others in your hardship is for you to be a help to others in their hardships. Paul gave help to the churches, and received help too.

Reach out and strengthen old relationships and be a blessing to others, and you will receive in return at least twofold what you put in.

Give and get help during your hardship.

Prayer to the Lord

> *Lord Jesus, I need your help. I am not able to carry the burdens of life alone; my strength is insufficient. But your strength, oh Lord, is sufficient. Carry my burdens for me, Lord. Send help. Bring people into my life who can partner with me in my hardship, and help me too to be a blessing to those around me. May the hands and feet of Christ, the body of Christ, work in and through me, oh Lord.*

> *In Jesus' name, Amen.*

Question to Consider

> *Who from your past could be an encouragement to you as well being encouraged by you?*

Day 59

All We Need

Philippians 4:19

My God will supply all your needs according to his riches in glory in Christ Jesus.

This verse is a promise that God will supply all that we need when we are battling cancer, and in all other trials of life. Let's explore each part of it....

God supplies according to the riches of his glory

God desires the name of Jesus to be glorified. God, by definition, is glorious, and his purposes work to bring glory to his name, which he rightly deserves. Specifically, he works to bring glory to himself through "the riches of his glory on objects of mercy that he prepared beforehand for glory—on us, the ones he also called" (Romans 9:23).

This mercy will result in our physical healing, either in this life or the next. But the most important gift of mercy is the covering of our sins by the blood of Jesus. This forgiveness is our greatest need, all other needs are secondary. And yet God is so gracious that he supplies those other needs too; he supplies *all* that is needed to glorify his Son Jesus Christ in and through our lives.

God supplies all we need to glorify him

Sometimes what brings God the most glory is our healing in this life, and God supplies it. Sometimes what brings God the most glory is our dying and returning home to him, because his good work in us is complete (Philippians 1:6). The completion of that good work, when seen end-to-end, is a masterpiece painted by none other than God, and we marvel at his handiwork.

All of God's provision has that same intended outcome; he supplies our needs so that he would get glory for the name of Christ Jesus. That should be your goal, too. You should "seek first the kingdom of God and his righteousness, and all these things will be provided for you" (Matthew 6:33).

This is how and why God works in us.

Praise the name of Christ Jesus, therefore, for all that he supplies! Tell of the good works of God in your life to all those who will lend an ear to listen! Tell everyone of the hope you have in Christ Jesus!

Prayer to the Lord

> *Father God, grant unto me, by your grace and mercy, all that I need to glorify the name of Christ Jesus in and through my journey with cancer. I pray, in the powerful name of Jesus, that I would be healed of this cancer. But, just as the Lord Jesus himself said, "Not my will be done, oh Lord, but your will be done in me." Your will is the glory of the riches of mercy in and through Jesus for me. Hear my cries for mercy, oh Lord. Glorify your Son Jesus through my life.*
>
> *In Jesus' name, Amen.*

Question to Consider

> *Reflect on a time in your life when God gave you something you needed and you gave God the glory for having received it.*

Day 60

To God be the Glory Forever

Philippians 4:20

Now to our God and Father be glory forever and ever. Amen.

This verse is a fitting end to our 60 days of reflection on the goodness of God in the midst of cancer. We've seen how the Lord draws near to us in our time of need, and how he pushes away fear by holding us with his righteous right hand (Isaiah 41:10, 13). We've seen how God has given us a spirit of power, love, and sound judgment, and how we're not beholden to a spirit of fear (2 Timothy 1:7). We've seen how God has a good plan for our lives, and how *he* will carry us until its completion (Philippians 1:6). We have seen how we'll be clothed with new bodies in the resurrection (Philippians 3:20-4:1). We've seen so many great and wonderful truths and promises of God to give us hope and courage in our fight with cancer.

And now we see what all this is for. All of God's help and provision for us is for our greatest joy to be sure (James 1:2-4), but more supremely, it is for the glory of God, which is best seen when we trust him in our deepest time of need.

Glory is an interesting thing to ponder. Our first inclination is to resist the glorification of an any individual, seeing that as pridefulness or narcissism. So how can it be good for God to seek his own glory, in particular seeking his glory in our suffering? Isn't that evil of God? How can that be good?

We know God cannot sin (1 John 3:5) and there's no evil in God. The Bible tells us this, and so we must trust it. However, it also bears up under scrutiny. An analogy I once heard can help us here:

There were two generals, one evil and the other good.

203

The evil general sacrificed countless thousands of his troops to win a battle that could have been won through negotiated peace. He commanded the troops into action so that he would get much glory and praise for defeating the enemy. Indeed, the general gloated much over his victory. This was self-glorification at the expense of others.

The good general, on the other hand, knew the desperate plight of his army. He knew of their certain defeat because of their weariness from endless battle. He knew that only he himself could lead them into battle and boost their morale. So this great general led the troops at the center of the vanguard, where the fighting was most severe. He knew he wouldn't survive, but because of his love for his men and his nation, he led them nonetheless. He died in that battle, but not before dealing the decisive blow to the enemy. His sacrifice saved not only his troopers, but also his entire nation, because the enemy was utterly defeated. Therefore his nation forever memorializes his likeness, giving glory to the general always.

God is like the second general. God understood the plight of his sinful people. He knew that only he could pay the price for their sin, and so he himself came to earth and dwelt among us and sacrificed himself on the cross for us. We the people of God therefore joyfully glorify God in Christ Jesus for his sacrificial love, because even while we were helpless sinners, and even enemies of God, Christ died for us (Romans 5:6-11).

There is no downside to God seeking to glorify the name of Christ Jesus. We praise the name of Jesus because of the certain hope of salvation we have in him and the thankfulness we have for his life-giving sacrifice. We praise Jesus for his Spirit, who gives us strength to endure through difficult circumstances such as cancer. It would be unthinkable, in fact, *not* to praise the name of Jesus given all he has done, is doing, and will do for us.

To God be the glory in our battle with cancer, because his Spirit sustains us. To Christ be the glory in our healing, because ultimately it is he who heals us, whether through the wisdom provided to doctors or through the gift of perfect bodies on the day of the Lord.

All things are from Christ and to Christ and through Christ;

to Christ Jesus be the glory forever.

God created you to seek and display Christ Jesus' glory. It is why you exist. It is your purpose, your identity. So display the glory of Jesus to others in and through your cancer.

Prayer to the Lord

Lord Jesus, I worship you! I praise your name! For in your power you defeated the enemy and saved me! In your name is power and might and majesty forever! To you, oh Lord, not me, be all glory, honor, and praise.

In Jesus' name, Amen.

Question to Consider

The majesty of God as seen in the glory of Christ Jesus is the supreme characteristic of God on display in the universe, but it is not the only characteristic of God. God is like a diamond with many facets, with the glory of Christ Jesus at the center. What other facets of God have shone brightly to light your way through dark valleys?

Epilogue

Fight the Good Fight

We've learned through the Scriptures in this book that a life of faith is a fight (1 Timothy 6:12). We are not passive or inactive, but engaged in an intentional fight against the forces of darkness and the worldly enticements that always fail us in the end.

Shortly after my diagnosis, my 12-year-old son wanted to know how to not be sad. He wanted to know how to fight the fight of faith. Entire books have been written on this subject, but I distilled for him what I knew to the following techniques. We remind each other of them continually. Whenever we feel fear or sadness, we go to war with these techniques and are encouraged! I hope you will be, too. Don't succumb to the enemies of your soul; rather, war against them! Fight!

Pray to Jesus – We are told to pray without ceasing, and experience teaches me that this is the most powerful tool in our arsenal to fight against all kinds of darkness (1 Thessalonians 5:16-18).

Walk in gratitude to God – Fear is most commonly focused on the future. Gratitude, however, is rooted in the moment. Jesus tells us to live day-by-day and to not worry about tomorrow, and the best way I know to do that is to walk in gratitude to God. Fear cannot take root in your heart when you are overflowing in thankfulness to God for what he has done for you or who he is to you or what he will do for you in the future.

Read the Word of God – Seek and find the promises of God for you; hear God speaking to you individually and personally through his Holy Bible. Consider creating some flash cards of some of your favorite verses and commit them to memory. In an instant of fear, having a verse or two at the tip of your tongue is a powerful weapon.

Worship God – For me this meant having praise and worship music playing in our house nearly constantly; when feelings of sadness or fear arose, there was always a gentle reminder playing in the background to turn to Jesus. See the Appendix for a list of songs that encouraged me powerfully through my early days of cancer.

Give somebody a hug – Pursue Christian community. The hands and feet of Christ Jesus are his church. Pursue Jesus' church and be comforted, and comfort others also. With the love God has for you, love others likewise.

Journal the truths and promises you believe – I was never a journaler before getting cancer, but when you get that diagnosis, you are desperate for the promises of God. I wrote those promises down because I needed to remind myself of them continually. Journaling also helped me to face my feelings in an age where we use Netflix and video games to run away from feeling anything. Consider adding journaling into your daily routine.

Finally, it seems fitting to me to end with an example of someone who fought this fight of faith in the midst of physical ailments. Martha Snell Nicholson suffered chronic pain from four diseases her entire life, and yet she was a prolific Christian poet. Her poem _The Thorn_ is the perfect conclusion to and summary of this book.

The Thorn

I stood a mendicant of God before His royal throne
And begged him for one priceless gift, which I
    could call my own.

I took the gift from out His hand, but as I would
depart
I cried, "But Lord this is a thorn and it has pierced
my heart.
This is a strange, a hurtful gift, which Thou hast
given me."
He said, "My child, I give good gifts and gave My
best to thee."
I took it home and though at first the cruel thorn
hurt sore,
As long years passed I learned at last to love it more
and more.
*I learned He never gives a thorn without this added
grace,*
*He takes the thorn to pin aside the veil which hides
His face.*

by Martha Snell Nicholson (emphasis added)

Afterword

On the day I learned of my tumor, the Lord put in my mind a book I had never read but which had a title that is hard to forget. The book was *Don't Waste Your Cancer* by John Piper. It's a short book, and I figured the day of diagnosis was as good a time as any to read it.

For some reason or another, the book (and my experiences with cancer, obviously) lit a fire in my heart for my legacy to my children. I knew, given their young age, there were expressions of my faith that I could not fully communicate to them. But I desperately wanted to.

So I started writing.

I'd never journaled before, and yet the outcome of this journaling was an entire book.

I hope, trust, and pray, in Jesus' name, that I have not, nor will be found to have, wasted my cancer. I want as many people as possible to know the hope I have in Christ Jesus. This was, is, and always will be my prayer first to my family, second to my church, and finally, if the Lord wills, perhaps even to many whom I will not meet until heaven.

Prayer to the Lord

> *Oh Lord God, help me not to waste my cancer. Give me opportunities, Jesus, to share the hope I have in you to anybody who will listen. May my ordeal bring the name of Jesus much glory and open to me new measures of joyful contentment I never thought possible.*
>
> *In your name Jesus I pray, to you be the glory, and not me, for you are sustaining me, always.*
>
> *Amen.*

Appendix

Songs that Encourage Me

I created a YouTube Music playlist called "The Lord got me through this." Below is a list of songs that encouraged my heart during my fiery trial:

- Way Maker - Leeland
- 10,000 Reasons - Matt Redman
- Break Every Chain - Jesus Culture
- Forever - Bethel Music
- Lord, I Need You - Matt Maher
- In Christ Alone - Adrienne Liesching
- King of My Heart - Steffany Gretzing
- Build my Life - Pat Barrett
- Even If - MercyMe
- Cornerstone - Hillsong Worship
- Who You Say I Am - Hillsong Worship
- Oceans (Where My Feet May Fail) - Hillsong United
- God, You're So Good - Passion
- Raise a Hallelujah - Jonathan David Helser
- Your Love Never Fails - Jesus Culture
- Break Every Chain - Tasha Cobbs Leonard
- In Jesus' Name (God of Possible) - Katy Nichole
- Let it Rain - Michael W. Smith
- I Speak Jesus - Here Be Lions
- Reckless Love - Cory Asbury
- Spirit Lead Me - Influence Music
- Nothing Else - Cody Carnes
- Surrounded - Bethel Music
- Raise a Hallelujah - Bethel Music

Acknowledgements

First and foremost, I want to thank the Lord for making this book possible. I know it sounds cliché, but honestly God gets the glory for this book and all the "good" that has come from my diagnosis. As I write this it's been eight months since my diagnosis, and while the future remains uncertain, as it is for us all, I have never been more certain in the faithfulness of God. Lord, thank you for your faithfulness! Use this book, Lord, for your good purposes and build up your church. In Jesus' name, Amen.

I also must acknowledge my wife Sarah in this work. She more than anybody has walked with me powerfully in prayer and in deed, and much of what I said in this book she first said to me in words of encouragement. Likewise, I acknowledge the many prayers of my parents, my mother-in-law, my sisters, the many drivers who drove me three hours round trip for chemo/radiation treatment daily for five weeks, and countless others' prayers who helped make this possible. The power of their prayers and words of encouragement cannot be understated. Where did the astonishing hope that I have, from which this book was written, come from? Not from me, but from the Lord through the power of the prayers of his saints. Thank you!

Lastly, I want to thank my publisher The Way With Words and my editor Dave Swavely. Every page of this book was filled with red ink, which only speaks to my desperate need for an editor and Dave's wonderful giftedness as one. There should be no doubt that Dave leveled up the quality and impact of this book in an immeasurable way. Thank you.

About Phil

Phil Wicklund is just a regular guy, desperately clinging to Jesus, who was diagnosed with esophageal cancer at age 40. He is married to Sarah Wicklund, has five children, and lives in Minneapolis, MN, where he attends Sanctuary Covenant Church, and works at Google as a Product Manager.

Connect with Phil at AstonishingHope.org.

Made in the USA
Monee, IL
01 June 2025